WORD AND SPIRIT

WORD
AND
SPIRIT

a monastic review

16

THE MONASTERY AND THE CITY

ST. BEDE'S PUBLICATIONS
Petersham, Massachusetts

Copyright © 1994 by St. Bede's Publications
All Rights Reserved
PRINTED IN THE UNITED STATES OF AMERICA

Published with ecclesiastical permission

Word and Spirit is a monastic review published once a year.
Ordinarily each issue focuses on a single theological or spiritual
theme, or commemorates some significant event in the history of
Christianity.

Articles appearing in this journal are abstracted and indexed in
Religious and Theological Abstracts. *Word and Spirit* is also available
in microform from University Microfilms International, 300
North Zeeb Road, Ann Arbor, MI 48106.

The Library of Congress has cataloged this serial title as follows:

Word and spirit. — 1-   St. Bede's Publications,
    c1979-

        v.; 22 cm.
    Annual.
    "A monastic review."
    Cover title: Word & Spirit
    ISSN 0193-9211 = Word and spirit.

    1. Catholic Church—Periodicals.   2. Theology—Periodicals.
3. Monasticism and religious orders—Periodicals.   I. Titles:
Word & spirit.

BX801.W67   282   81-643362
ISBN 1-879007-10-X [vol. 16]

Published by: St. Bede's Publications
            P.O. Box 545
            Petersham, MA 01366-0545

Contents

WORD AND SPIRIT

A PLACE WHERE VIRTUE MAY BE MAGNIFIED: THE CITY, THE POLIS AND THE MONASTERY

Judith Sutera, OSB
(*Mount St. Scholastica,
Atchison, Kansas*)
and
Deborah Vess
(*DeKalb College,
Dunwoody, Georgia*)

Christian literature is filled with images of the community of the faithful as a city. In the *Life of Antony* attributed to Athanasius, the "desert was made a city by monks who left their own people and registered themselves for citizenship in the heavens."[1] Augustine spoke of the "City of God" as transcending the rise and fall of earthly "Cities of Babylon." But what makes the image of the city so meaningful? What is a city meant to be and what has it been historically?

Lewis Mumford's *The City in History: Its Origins, Its Transformations and Its Prospects* remains the classic exposition of the origin and character of the city. Mumford traces the origin of the city to the human need for physical and spiritual fulfillment. The city began as a place where people might express common religious beliefs, preserve the memory of their dead, and enhance their chances for survival. On a purely practical level, the city was a place where one might optimize the use of shared natural resources. Yet the spiritual needs of humans ultimately were of as much or even more importance in the evolution of the city than were the purely physical needs. Two of the original three purposes of the city arose out of spiritual concerns. The first cities were built around sites of humankind's earliest expressions of religious sentiment. The paleolithic caves, laced with magical art, were an attempt to convey divine power over the physical realm. Prehistoric cave art symbolized human triumph over the animal world, if only momentarily, as well as human permanence and continuation.[2]

From the paleolithic cave to the Athenian acropolis, religious needs dictated the climate of politics. The city in its primordial form was intended as a place where humans could reach their fullest potential, where their highest selves were expressed in community with others of similar beliefs. The primitive city was a ceremonial center,

> an association dedicated to a life more abundant: not merely an increase of food, but an increase of social enjoyment, through the fuller use of fantasy and art, with a shared vision of a better life, one meaningful as well as esthetically enchanting.[3]

As the city evolved, however, these early ideals were corrupted, for the growth of human settlement brought with it human diversity. Diversity bred struggles for power, power which was ultimately divested in monarchs, creating new divisions between governors and those governed. The quest for power between civilizations with differing goals and beliefs was often resolved on the battlefield. The struggle for supremacy, whether within or without the city, gradually devoured the ideological underpinnings of the city, and transformed it from a place where the individual might reach his or her fullest potential to a place where the individual was subjugated to the needs and desires of those privileged few in power. Although the city contained within its walls the potential to magnify the quality of life, it also paradoxically contained the seed of its own demise. "Is it merely by chance that the earliest images of the city... picture its destruction?"[4]

Yet throughout the course of human civilization, there have been those who have hearkened back to the ideals of the early city, urging society to reclaim its original sense of community. The social visions of both Aristotle and St. Benedict of Nursia were attempts to create communities "dedicated to a life more abundant."

The Greek Polis

Aristotle's philosophy was rooted in the Greek concept of the *polis*. The ancient Greeks promoted a commonwealth where reason and science were permeated with a deep sense of ethics and morality. The Greek *polis* is the basis of modern western society, and embedded in the meaning of the term itself is the very essence of Greek government. The word *polis* originally denoted the acropolis, or the seat of government in the community, but as the meaning evolved, it came to be applied to the country dwellers who frequented the community, as well as to the citizens who lived around the acropolis. Later, *polis* also designated a power engaged in relations with another power. Thus, the word came to mean the entire community working together, as opposed to denoting merely the governing bodies.

One of the most important ancient analyses of various ways in which such a *polis* might function was Aristotle's *Politics*. Aristotle's conception of politics was far different from that of the modern era, for in Aristotle's world, politics was intimately fused with ethics. Ethics did not transcend politics, but was an integral part of political theory. Aristotle's ideal *polis* was permeated by his concept of ethical behavior, and the chief function of the *polis* was to instill morality in its citizens. Life in a *polis* was the most natural way for humans to exist, for all human existence reached perfection in the *polis*. It was there that humankind achieved its true end, *eudaimonia*, or well-being. *Eudaimonia* was understood by Aristotle as "the energy and practice of goodness, to a degree of perfection, and in a mode which is absolute and not relative."[5] This practice of goodness led to moral perfection. Well-being could not be attained through the use and possession of physical goods, but was achieved primarily through the attributes of a moral soul. Although it has often been translated as "happiness," *eudaimonia* was not simply a static condition but a continuous expression of morality through action. The *polis* was the only place where people could achieve this end, as *eudaimonia* could not be cultivated in solitude. Life in community was the means by which humankind realized its very nature, and the virtuous life led in an Aristotelian *polis* was perfection of each individual.

The *Politics* was thus an expression of the spirit of ancient Greeks. The *Politics*, however, cannot be read in isolation, but was the culmination of Aristotle's theory of virtue as set forth in the *Nicomachaen Ethics*. Here, virtue was defined as a disposition to act in accordance with a mean between two extremes, where actions were determined by such rational principles as a person of wisdom would employ.[6] Aristotle did not believe that people were born virtuous; rather, virtue must be cultivated through the practice of right action. Virtue thus involved practical knowledge as well as theoretical insight. This view of human virtue as a disposition of the soul to be cultivated was transformed in the *Politics* into a way of life in which the Greek ideals of balance and harmony were implanted into the very fabric of society.

The *polis* was not simply a place where virtue may be magnified, but the only place where human beings could achieve the end for which they were created. The *Politics* was the finest expression of Aristotle's vision of the community as the realization of the deepest truths known to humankind. The *polis* was a place where religion and politics were not separate but aspects of the same living reality. It was a place where the soul found spiritual fulfillment, in which its actions as a political being were synonymous with its moral perfection. Aristotle's vision of the *polis* as a center for spiritual development was one of the most important contributions of the ancient Greeks.

The Benedictine Monastery as Polis

This insight into the enduring value of the city was also one of the foundations of the monastic tradition. From the earliest literature of the desert, the monastery was referred to as a city. By its very nature, a monastic community is a gathering of persons with common beliefs using shared resources. In his synthesis of monastic tradition, Benedict of Nursia came to many of the same conclusions as had Aristotle centuries before.

Aristotle argued that the nature of a *polis* limited its size. Although Aristotle never articulated a rationale for this position, other historians such as Mumford have argued that the ideal city should be limited in size. The *polis* was thought of as a self-sufficient community, whose size was limited to the number of people it could comfortably support. If the group became too large, communication would be hampered and the sense of fellowship destroyed. Unless interaction could occur on a regular basis, it would not be possible for individuals to bond with all members of the community. Consequently, the social fabric would dissolve and the result would be strife, corruption, and a sense of remoteness from those in power and from the decision-making process.

The Rule demonstrates that Benedict also recognized the necessity of self-sufficiency and ongoing communication between the inhabitants of the monastic city. The monastery was envisioned as a place where all necessities would be contained within its walls. Although Benedict did not stipulate the ideal size for a community, he provided for smaller divisions to improve organization and communication, whenever the number of members was "rather large." Throughout the ages, monastic communities have maintained communication by such methods as daily chapter meetings, in which the day's activities and any community business are discussed with all members. In a Benedictine community, major decisions involve a listening process which includes consulting even the youngest members of the community.

Mumford argued that as the city grew and became more complex, its original aims were perverted by the struggle for power. Benedict's Rule preserved the spirit of the early city because it envisioned a group of people working for the common good, disinterested in personal power. The monastery was to be led by a person selected for "goodness of life and wisdom in teaching" and one who is guided by the interest of the community as opposed to personal gain.

A person with these qualities will not be a tyrant, but will be fair, flexible and just. Just as Aristotle believed that law should adapt itself to particular circumstances, Benedict was careful to remind his readers frequently that different living conditions required different responses. His principles were meant to serve as a guide for future experience rather than as inflexible rules which were to be applied to every person and case. The monastic leader was not to be an autocrat, but one who would take into consideration the needs and opinions of a variety of people with differing characteristics. The burden in a monastic community rested not only with the leader, but with each individual.

One of the key virtues for living the monastic life is obedience, and Benedict stressed that this is owed by each person to every other person. Promotion of the common good results from the mandate that "no one is to pursue what he judges best for himself, but instead, what he judges better for someone else." Such a community working together realizes the true meaning of the word *polis* as the sum of the entire community.

In fact, the model for both the *polis* and the monastery was the family. Aristotle traced the origin of the community back to the need for survival and security, and found its first manifestation in the family unit. Benedict also looked to the family as a meaningful analogy for the monastic life. The leader was to be "devoted and tender as a parent," and the monastics were to love one another "with the pure love of brothers and sisters." The most important function of the monastic leader was to promote the spiritual development of the community members, a concept that recalls the very heart of Aristotle's *Politics*. In an Aristotelian *polis*, virtue must be carefully cultivated and nurtured. One of the most important functions of the Benedictine leader was to be a teacher who modeled right behavior. The superior must be the epitome of virtue, for he or she takes the place of Christ in the monastery "leading more by example than by word." Others in a position of leadership, such as the deans, were also instructed to serve as role models. The eighth step of humility, in fact, lists two measures of obedience: a monastic is bound both to the common rule and to the example set by superiors.

The monastic also is to learn virtue through monastic practices which foster the interior disposition. Chapter 4 of the Rule begins the list of tools for good works by listing actions which are based on the commandments and the imitation of the life of Jesus. Performance of these good deeds is only one dimension of good works, while virtuous inner qualities comprise the latter part of the list.

A sense of progression from outer deed to inner disposition is captured in the twelve steps of humility. One begins by acting in a way which fosters humility and gradually moves to an internal honesty. This realization leads to strengthening of action, but with deeper and more spiritual motivation. In the twelfth step, the outer actions of the monastic are the result of an inner disposition which prefers nothing whatever to the love of Christ. Although the outer actions are essentially the same, the intensity is greater; they have been transformed, so that now they are performed naturally and spontaneously.

At the same time the monastic is in the process of personal conversion, the practices of daily living, such as prayer, work, common table, and shared goods force individuals to become a corporate entity. In discovering the diversity of personalities in the monastery, and learning the personal skills needed to blend them into a cohesive whole, each individual's self-discovery is enhanced. The process of personal conversion is altered and tempered because the common good becomes part of one's value system. In community, one's personal good must be subordinated to the common good, and this deepens the individual's growth in humility. The monastic realizes dependence on God through dependence on community.

True conversion occurs when the interior disposition transforms all action, while action is simultaneously transforming the interior, harmonizing the inner and outer life of the monastic. Benedict spiritualized the meaning of *polis*, for the monastic becomes an embodiment of the common good, desiring nothing else and submitting to the will of the community as well as to the superior. The monastic literally becomes the *polis* and the *polis* the monastic. The city was originally intended to be a place where one might maximize one's inner potential. The spirituality of a Benedictine monastery attempts to fuse individual and community to such a degree that even individual salvation is incomplete unless all are brought together to everlasting life.

The Rule is an integrated and multi-layered spiritual guide which illuminates a path towards moral perfection, but that path is never-ending. At the end of the Rule, Benedict indicated that all that had preceded was merely a beginning. The monastic life is a daily turning toward God, a renewal of commitment to heeding and responding to the word of God. Even the seemingly linear steps of humility were perceived by Benedict as a constant process, for they were likened to the ascent and descent of the angels on the ladder of Jacob.

This continuous spiritual growth captured the Aristotelian concept of "nature." Aristotle argued that the nature of a thing was its final end, its state of perfection. For humans, the final end was *eudaimonia* or well-being. The nature of a person is thus not how the person is born, but the realization of the perfection peculiar to one's species. The Greek word for "nature" can refer to either the process of growth, the growth itself, or the beginning of growth. This suggests that the nature of a person for Aristotle was not a static state, but a potentiality which is progressively realized throughout the course of human existence.

Benedict's *conversatio morum suorum* is a similarly rich term, implying the current state of an individual as well as his or her continuous progression in spirituality. It is a way of life, not a simple set of customs, that one cultivates in an environment which fosters such growth. Aristotle presented virtue in the *Ethics* as a disposition; as he grew in the contemplative life himself, he came to view it in the *Politics* as a way of life. The Benedictine monastery is an Aristotelian *polis*, in which the monastic may realize the true end of human nature as Benedict sees it: eternal life in the fullness of the kingdom.

As attractive as Aristotle's concept of *eudaimonia* might appear, Aristotle was at heart a scientist who approached human nature through the techniques and methodologies of the scientist. For Aristotle, virtuous action was action which a rational person of wisdom would choose. One acted in a virtuous way because it was in one's own best interest. He catalogued virtue, as well as the virtuous *polis*, in the same manner in which a scientist would catalogue the genera and species of plant and animal life. Although Aristotle portrayed contemplation as the highest goal of humanity, he never quite seemed able to achieve contemplative union with the divine. Unlike Plato, he did not subscribe to the world of forms, a divine and unchanging world accounting for all experience. Aristotle was a pragmatist who preferred to explain experience in terms of the world around him. In so doing, he lost touch with one of the basic desires of humanity, the need for a transcendent God who is nevertheless immanent in the world of experience.

Benedict shared many of the same presuppositions as Aristotle, yet fully integrated his *polis* with an awe-inspiring sense of divinity. His monastic city was truly the City of God, already partially present through the life of Christ, yet still to be fully realized in the end time. Benedict captured a sense of eternity and made it ever present to the monastic through a continuous process of spiritual growth. Actions in the monastic city foreshadow the life in the peaceable kingdom, and thus God is not something far removed but the true ruler of the monastery.

Although the city was originally formed to fulfill humanity's longing for the sacred, the growth of cities and the rise of power centers ultimately corrupted these early ideals. Historians and social scientists attribute the malaise of modern society to the individual's inability to find fulfillment in the modern city, which has expanded to the point that individuals become mere statistics to be used or abused by the power infrastructure. Communities are no longer tight-knit expressions of common beliefs and goals, but conglomerations of diverse customs and traditions.

The cooperative nature of the early city, both for survival and for the expression of basic common emotions in worship, no longer exists in society. Modern technology has removed the contemporary urban dweller from the survival process and from the ongoing dialogue with nature and with the needs of other people. Mumford argues that modern perversions of the early city make it impossible for humanity to reach its fullest potential, and are the exact opposite of the city's original intent.

Benedictinism today stands as a living testament to the ideals and purpose of the early city. For fifteen hundred years, Benedictines have worked to unite the human with the divine, to ensure that humanity does not forget its origins. Benedictine life, when it is authentically lived, retains its connection with nature and its sense of responsibility and community with all of creation. Primacy is given to human interaction and personal development over function and production.

As seen from this perspective, the monastery ceases to appear isolated from the world, but rather captures the essential features of some of the finest thought on the nature of civilization. It truly is a city unto itself, even when it is no longer materially self-sufficient. It is a place where cooperative action has not been lost, but where people cooperate for spiritual as well as physical nourishment.

The monastery is the direct descendant of the sacred cave, where one ate and was sheltered with one's kin, buried and remembered the dead, and called down the divine powers. It was here that the forces of the universe were gathered into one tiny place and energized the lives of those present.

Society has lost much of the sense of mystery and vulnerability the cave dweller must have experienced. It has lost unity with nature; it has lost the unity of the prehistoric tribe. One contemporary author has pointed out that modern society is episodic, while monastic communities provide their members with a continuous narrative line.[7] As such, Benedictine monasticism unites past and present while simultaneously calling forth the future. It is a future which still carries with it the hopes of humanity, the desire for the divine and a sense that these two goals are one.

NOTES

1. Athanasius, *The Life of Anthony* (New York: Paulist Press, 1980), 42-43.

2. Lewis Mumford, *The City in History: Its Origins, Its Transformations, and Its Prospects* (New York: Harcourt, Brace and World, 1961), chapter 1.

3. *Ibid.*, 8.

4. *Ibid.*, chapter 2.

5. *Ibid.*, VII, xiii, 5, 312.

6. Aristotle, *Nicomachean Ethics*, in *The Basic Works of Aristotle*, ed. Richard McKeon (New York: Random House, 1941), II, vi, 959.

7. Mary Jo Leddy, Interview in *The American Monastic Newsletter*, vol. 21, no. 2, June 1991.

CITY AND DESERT IN MONASTIC THEOLOGY

David Foster
*(Downside Abbey,
Bath, England)*

The desert and city stand in opposition to each other. The contrast is characteristic both of modern and of ancient civilization, and its position in Christian spirituality fundamental.[1] The wilderness, and withdrawal into it, has often been seen as the peculiar characteristic of monastic life, not only as a rejection of the pagan city whose society was felt to be organized opposition to God, but also of the Christian city, with its earthly distractions from uninterrupted converse with God.[2]

Nonetheless the monastery and city have not always been seen antithetically. Augustine, in particular, has been presented as one who brought the monastery into the city,[3] and there were monasteries in towns before that, such as the one founded by Eusebius of Vercelli for his clergy, or the ones in Rome where Augustine himself received his initial first-hand experience of Christian monastic life.[4] In Latin Christendom the urban monastery and the part played by the monastery as the center of economic and civic life in missionary territories has been indebted to Augustine, and the very organization of the large monasteries involved in this work took on, in a number of instances, some of the features and ethos of a city.

The relationship is an ambiguous one. The controversial implications of this in a town like York, for example, led to the foundation of the Cistercian monastery at Fountains Abbey.[5] In the modern world, or the parts of it where Christian monasticism has been most firmly established, and which is dominated by the heavily urbanized culture of modernity, the relation of monastery to the culture of the city is a pressing question. The following study is directed at some of the implications of the relationship between monastery and city suggested by the monastic thought of Augustine, in the light of some recent discussions of monastic origins.

Augustine's monasticism has been said to lie at the parting of the ways. Previously monks had turned to the desert because it was not possible to live the full Christian life in towns. Christian life meant to the first monks a life spent fighting the demons in their desert habitat; for this reason it was a life of self-denial, an ascetic life. Although the growing identification of the Church with the world in the fourth century meant that the orientation towards the desert of the desire for perfection was never superseded, Augustine brought the monastery more closely into relation with the life of the city.[6]

Augustine's own path to monastic life was certainly distinctive.[7] His debt to classical culture along this path, not least the ideal of philosophy and the *otium* to go with it, is evident and has been amply studied.[8] Augustine had certainly come to this ideal through his experience of friendship, and his longing for it.[9] His classical education gave him, too, a deep appreciation of literature and of the rhetorical qualities which distinguished it.

But, however distinctive, and distinctively marked by the culture of the Roman *civitas*, this path has much in common with the path that took monks before Augustine into the desert. It was hearing of the monastic life inspired by the *Life of Antony* which Christians in Trier were living that turned out to be the last straw needed to break Augustine's resistance, a moral resistance, to Baptism.[10] The language he uses, for example his use of the expression *servire deo*, is a strong indication of his interpreting the process of conversion in terms taken from traditional Christian asceticism.[11] The community he founded at Thagaste, moreover, has not always been seen as a monastery in the proper sense, but such evidence as there is points very much in that direction. It was a far cry from the aristocratic *otium* of Cassiciacum, where everything was subordinated to the ends of philosophical discourse.[12]

Augustine's debt to this tradition of desert monasticism invites further attention. Moreover, research into monastic origins in Egypt has shed light on an interest there in community for which Augustine is so clearly celebrated. It gives a further reason to be a little hesitant about drawing too fundamental a contrast between their respective approaches to monastic life.

Several factors lie behind the development, or emergence, of monastic forms of asceticism.[13] As an eremitical movement, monasticism has been considered primarily in relation to the individual monk's spiritual search. Etymology has played its part too in considering what it was to be a monk or a hermit.[14] But when the hermit is looked at more from the outside and from a sociological point of view, social factors in his motivation come into play.[15]

P. Brown suggests that people were driven into the desert by a "crisis in human relations" caused by the economic and social developments in fourth century Egypt, combined with the burden of taxation, which widened social divisions between villagers and put the traditional ties of mutual support under strain. The anchorite was someone who cut himself loose from the normal social means of establishing his identity in order to find his true self. But he did not thereby lose his relevance to the society he had left.[16] Brown links the incoherence felt by the monk in his own existence to the larger incoherence of increasingly unmanageable social conditions in Christian communities.[17] By going into the desert, the monk sought to face up to all this. Introspection, and confrontation with the supernatural world, enabled him to face up to the demonic powers of the *saeculum*.

Not only has the relationship of the monk to the society he abandoned been the subject of study, but also the relationships which thereby came into existence between monks, however loosely organized they were by the standards of full-fledged cenobitic life.[18] Graham Gould, for instance, has focused on the specific ways reflected in the *Apophthegmata* by which desert monks sought to establish an alternative society. He speaks of "the creation of a new community, a new social ideal."[19]

> What is important...is that this renunciation of society, this search for *autarky* and social "death" was not an individual quest.... In the relationships between their members and in the institution of the *agape* the communities possessed a means of cohering into an identifiable group, the forum of

an extended, community-wide discussion of the problems of the monastic life and the basis of a consensus on the relative importance of solitude and of relationships. In the teaching relationship the community possessed a means of renewing itself and of transmitting information about its history over the generations.[20]

Gould also argues that these more or less informal structures accommodated various degrees of solitude and community so that the categories he employs could explain cenobitic as well as eremitic forms of monasticism.

This approach is a valuable corrective to one which places an emphasis on the individual monk exclusive of other considerations, and to the consequent tendency to criticize them for an individualistic, competitive spirituality.[21] In particular, it makes it hard to make the contrast between solitude and community, between hermitage and cenobium, map precisely onto the contrast between desert and city.[22]

The desert gave people an environment empty enough to try to redefine how the community and individual relate. A community in the ancient world, a *polis*, gave someone their identity; it was fixed by one's family and birth with little opportunity for social mobility. The Late Empire made it even harder, while the crisis in civic life of the time also made it hard to establish that sense of identity with any satisfaction by means of a sense of participating usefully in the society on which it depended. The Roman world was a jigsaw of such civic units, apart from a few client kingdoms, and tribes. The rest was desert. The desert was the place where no city could provide an *identikit*. The desert was by definition, therefore, useless in terms of social or economic interests which conditioned social function and personal identity as a result. But to say that it is therefore meaningless gives the lie to the way our sensitivity to nature is warped by the materialism inherent in human culture. A place without cultural meaning is where the only meaning it can have is its nature as such, its created meaning given by God.[23] The desert was a privileged place of encounter with God, where monks as well might be able to get back to their own createdness, their own real identity in the eyes of God.

In forcing a monk back on himself in order to find within himself the resources of personal identity, and the obstacles to living it out, a monk might hope to come face to face with his creator, on the one hand; but, on the other, he was forced to face up to the power of evil which disabled and corrupted his humanity. Simon Tugwell puts it as follows:

> What they all had in common was a quest for a definition of human life independent of any definitions contained in the ordinary structures of life.... The coming of Christ had re-opened the fundamental question, what it means for us to be human beings. It is no longer sufficient to accept from our social milieu the values, aspirations and so on which structure our concept of ourselves; the question has to be pushed to a much further limit: "What is a human being as such, as envisaged by the Creator?"
>
> It is difficult to avoid the feeling that at least some of the curious practices adopted by some ascetics were intended to be a kind of experiment, designed to extract further evidence of just what it is to be human...it is by pushing human nature to the limits of its endurance that you discover what human nature really is.[24]

But the emergence of fairly coherent forms of social patterns among the Desert Fathers can also be related to this understanding of the motivation of monastic life.[25] Monks were able to rediscover how human beings, aware of themselves, and of God, could relate well to each other. So the forms of monastic society which came into existence represent an interest in how human society might be grounded in the creativity of God, and strive to be free of the corrupting power of an alien culture. This is shown in their absorption in the scriptures, and in the centrality to monastic society of the relationship with a teacher, a living exponent of the Word. For the fundamental social relationship for the monk was that established for him by God in the word addressed to him. The same word brings human beings together to listen to it, and as fellows sharing the possibility of a new culture and a divine society opened up by the incarnation of the Word.[26]

To return to Augustine's interest in social relationships in a monastic community, there is a place in the prooemium to *De Doctrina Christiana* where the legendary Antony the Great is introduced.[27] At the outset of this work, Augustine anticipates various kinds of opposition to the project he has undertaken, in the course of which he will lay claim to the whole range of resources of human culture and deploy them in the service of understanding and communication of the Word. It is a manifesto for Augustine's appreciation of the city culture of his world. Antony is liable to be cited by critics because he was a man of the spirit and master of the Word without a classical education.

Here, then, is the desert monk being cited as a counter-example to Augustine's ideal of the *tractator scripturarum*. To deal with the objection, Augustine points out that human beings normally learn basic skills in comprehension and communication through a measure of socialization. For God has created the dispositions of human nature so as to be possessed by us by means of a shared culture, which God himself uses in saving and perfecting mankind. So, in the passage of *De Doctrina Christiana* already mentioned, Augustine says that the incarnation is the way, whereby God himself accustoms us to hear and understand the divine Word of salvation:

> So charity itself, who draws men together to himself in a knot of unity, would have no access to mens' souls to fill them and mix them, so to speak, with himself, if men learnt nothing from each other.[28]

Augustine's argument is a witness to the view that, for a social animal like man, the boundary between nature and culture is never clear.[29] It would therefore be wrong to reject culture out of hand, for it is the way human beings come into personal ownership of their natural birthright. But if the ambition to form a monastic society based on a rediscovery, and a redefinition, of human nature in terms of its graced createdness as such was an element in the motivation of the monastic movement, there was bound to be a certain ambivalence even in the desert towards culture. The critical point, though, was that monastic society and culture be centered on God's own initiative in the Incarnation, offering in Jesus Christ a new way of relating as human beings to each other.

This argument is important to understand both Augustine's appreciation of culture and his approach to monasticism. *De Doctrina Christiana* is remarkably generous to the classical heritage, much more so than monastic propaganda typically allowed. But even in this work, addressed to the needs of the Church at large, he is concerned no less than monks with the building up of wholesome social relations in the Christian community, based on the study and teaching of the Scriptures, which help to make Christ the basis of a Christian culture and society.[30]

Christ is the key to Augustine's love both of the classical philosophical culture and of the monastic ideal. He spent his life trying to find Christ at the center of classical culture; his early work shows an extraordinarily sophisticated way of trying to found the edifice of literary culture on a conception of Wisdom disclosing Christ, the Word made Flesh.[31] But it was important to make the transition from knowledge to wisdom; education in its fullest sense had its value in the discovery of Christ as the source of learning. Once Augustine had made that transition himself, it was no great step to take to see the resources of human culture as something to be devoted to expounding the knowledge of the divine mystery revealed in Scripture.[32]

Augustine's approach to culture is more tolerant, then, than that displayed by many monks and therefore puts a fundamental question to monasticism about the extent to which the quest for personal identity recreated in Christ, so central to the monastic ideal of the new creation, can only be appropriated by divesting oneself absolutely of one's education and inherited culture. There is indeed a contrast between Augustine and the radical renunciation of the desert monks. But it would be misleading to argue from this that he has changed the terms in which the monastic ideal is to be understood.[33] Augustine is concerned, no more than his Egyptian forebears, with authentic human society, and he sees as well as they did that what gives this authenticity is its differentiation from the *saeculum*, and its fellowship with Christ.

What is new in Augustine seems to be that the relation of personal and social, of solitude and cenobium, has been reversed. The essential motive and ideal of monastic life remain constant, but whereas the desert monk sought to recreate human relationships by learning to appropriate a new personal identity, Augustine sets the Christian community of the Church in first place as the environment in which a monk discovers his personal identity in Christ.[34] Reversing this relationship between personal and social does not make monastic asceticism redundant. Asceticism is still directed towards the appropriation by the individual of this new identity which the Church makes possible in Christ, and the priority which is given to realizing this at a personal level is what distinguishes the monk from fellow Christians in Augustine as much as before.

The Church is central to the novelty of Augustine's understanding of monasticism; it is able to play this part largely because of Augustine's own theological development of ecclesiology.[35] While the Church is essentially the heavenly society of the saints, its eschatological character is nevertheless combined with its actual state as a *corpus permixtum*, of wheat and tares. Argument with Donatists led Augustine to understand this; his reflection on Pelagianism led him to see that human reality itself exists on more than one level, both socially and personally, between an ideal and what is actual. No act of renunciation can free the Christian in this world from the mystery of sin *tout court*. For man's nature is as compromised as his culture. But the possibility of conversion and of tending by grace towards the real goal of existence in Christ makes possible too the reclaiming in him of culture.

In particular, it is his sacramental way of conceiving the new community of human relationships in the Church which gives Augustine's monastic thought a distinctive cast. The type of society which came into existence in the desert was essentially an educational one, based on teaching disciples at a very practical level how to live. The monastic community in Augustine is also a formative environment, but its social character is more that of being a model of the Church. If monastic life cannot free itself from the fallen condition of human nature, it can adopt a distinctive lifestyle, putting a particular priority on realizing the goal, and this gives it its special role to play within the Church.

The corollary of this is that the monk does not need to detach himself from the field of the Church's mission; indeed it has its own part to play within that mission as a witness after its own kind to the fullness of life to which all mankind is called within the Body of the Church. But beyond that, the strengthening of this sense of sharing in the mission of the Church permits a development in the way in which the monk sees his life as for others. The desert already presents evidence of a "social" motivation in the movement, especially in the way in which manual labor was justified; in Basil such a motivation became pre-eminent.[36] In Augustine, pastoral commitments of clerics are recognized as valid reasons for being exempted from monastic manual work.[37] The striking contribution made to the episcopal ministry of the Church in Africa by monks of his community, as that by the monks of Lérins who were more directly in the desert tradition mediated by Cassian, are both signs of the positive way in which monasticism as such discovered ways of sharing in the apostolic mission of the Church.[38]

It is impossible to understand Augustine's monastic theology without appreciating the way in which the Church mediates the person of Christ who is central to the monastic search. To understand his way of relating monastery and city, therefore, it is no less necessary to grasp his view of the way the Church provides a social environment mediating between Christ and human culture. It provides a way of making Christ present in that culture, and of attuning it to its proper goal in Christ. If the Incarnation enables a monk too to see positive links between the monastery and city, the theological character of the Church provides constraints on that relationship which should not be overlooked. First, there is a soteriological constraint, the need to see living in the world in terms of living for it, a sense of relationship between monastic life and the Church's mission. Second there is the eschatological constraint, the need to retain a vivid sense of the horizon of God's judgment before which all society stands. This has always been in the foreground of the monastic outlook. To be a reminder of it is an essential part of the role a monastery has to play in the Church. So if it is the Church's existence for the world mediating Christ as the "sacrament of encounter with God" which establishes its openness to the City of Man, it is likewise the Church's existence as the *civitas dei* which ensures the essential distinction from the world on which monasticism depends.[39]

Monasticism owes much to Augustine for the high value placed on human culture and artistic beauty especially in Latin Christianity, with all that it has done for the civilization of Christendom. But what monastic life has produced must not be mistaken for its motivation. The personal commitment of individual monks to making their own the humanity renewed by the person of Christ, and the representing of that person by each to all within whatever patterns of social relation define their life, with all the effort and self-discipline that costs, is what unites all monks with the aspiration of those who first left everything for the desert.

To extend the study of the relationship of the monastic tradition to the modern rather than the ancient city introduces some further considerations into the question. For the modern city is a far cry from the coherent, if stifling, cultural environment of the ancient world. T.S. Eliot, for example, uses the metaphor of the wilderness as the title of his poem on London after the Great War, *The Wasteland*. More recently A. MacIntyre's *After Virtue* has examined modernity on a broader front and argued that the crisis in the social coherence of the modern world cannot be isolated from a crisis in the ethical tradition of our culture. He sees a fragmentation of ethical communities which are isolated and vulnerable as a new Dark Age overtakes us.

Less melodramatically, he argues that what is needed is a revival of communities which will be adequate to recover a proper sense of ethics which he associates with Aristotle. He even speaks of the need for "another St Benedict."[40] There does indeed seem to be an interesting parallel between the crisis in urban and social life of the ancient world and the decision made by so many to drop out and try to find themselves in the desert. But the parallel also suggests that the monastic tradition does not set out in the first place to be such a cure for contemporary moral and social malaise. Nevertheless the results of the research mentioned here suggest some of the reasons why the monastic impulse is an important one in our day, particularly in its concern to get back to the basis of any social life, to recover a proper sense of human nature and the solidarity we enjoy by our nature as human beings with the creation as a whole. No less important is the conviction that this solidarity resides in a divine creative initiative, and that it is by committing oneself to the discovery of God through self-knowledge and the struggle with the hold of evil over one's nature, that the monk acquires a true sense of personal identity from his relationship with God.

For the modern tradition no longer seems able to educate people into a healthy sense of personal identity. It is the reason why social patterns seem merely conventional, and no longer to exercise any ethical authority. So the patterns of life within a monastic community and the way in which they create a field within which individuals can undertake responsibility for each other and find personal fulfillment in the shared tradition and project of the monastery may have nowadays a particular social value on a wider front. But the monastery will undermine the basis of its own existence if it sees its social life and culture only in secular terms, and fails to differentiate itself from the world in which it lives. So monasticism may indeed find a vocation towards the modern city; but it will be because the Church's mission there needs the distinctive sign of the monastic community. If the desert is nowadays to be found in the city and in its modern culture, it will be all the more necessary for monks in our day to be experienced in the wisdom of the desert where it came to birth.

NOTES

1. R. Williams, s.v. "Desert, Desert Fathers" in ed. G.S. Wakefield, *A Dictionary of Christian Spirituality*, London 1983; A. Louth, *The Wilderness of God*, London 1991.

2. See especially T. Wiedemann, "Polytheism, monotheism, and religious co-existence: Paganism and Christianity in the Roman Empire," in ed. I. Hamnett, *Religious Pluralism and Unbelief: Studies Critical and Comparative*, London 1990, 64-78, esp. 72-75. Also A. Momigliano, "Christianity and the Decline of the Roman Empire," in ed. *id.*, *The Conflict between Paganism and Christianity in the Fourth Century*, Oxford 1963, 11-13.

3. G. Lawless, *Augustine of Hippo and his Monastic Rule*, Oxford 1987.

4. Cf. Augustine, *De Moribus Ecclesiae Catholicae et de Moribus Manichaeorum*, I, xxxi, 66ff, xxxiii, 70: see Lawless' discussion, *Augustine* 42-43.

5. Its story has been made famous by M.D. Knowles, *Monastic Order in England. A History of its development from the times of St Dunstan to the Fourth Lateran Council, 940-1216*, Cambridge 1966[2].

6. R.A. Markus, *End of Ancient Christianity*, Cambridge 1990, 159-160, whose discussion of monasticism is fundamental to what follows, although I feel that it is an exaggeration to say that his achievement was to redefine the monastery "in terms which were essentially those of the city rather than the desert" (p. 160).

7. G. Lawless says that "Augustine's persevering response to a monastic calling...is possibly the most underrated facet of his personality," *Augustine*, 161. Augustine, *Confessions*, X, xiii, 70, presents a crux, where he admits to a yearning for the solitude of the desert which God talked him out of (as J.J. O'Donnell rather bluntly says in his *Commentary*, Vol. III, [Oxford 1992], 246); see A. Solignac's discussion in a note *ad loc.* in the French edition *BA 14* for views on the dating of this. It seems only to beg the question of the identity of monastic and solitary life.

8. This has normally been considered independently of monastic theology, ever since Marrou, in terms of the relationship between Christianity and classical culture in general. Specifically in terms of monasticism, Markus, *End*, 73-79, aligns Augustine with the classical ideal of the philosophic life; Lawless' study highlights the way that this classical tradition was used to interpret, but not to replace, a theological understanding of the experience of living together in Christ as a religious community. He also shows how the rhetoric of Roman political thought underpins his critique of the *saeculum* and his articulation by contrast of the social ideals of brotherhood and *concordia*.

9. Lawless, *Augustine*, 1: "Augustine was rarely alone."

10. Augustine, *Confessions* VIII, vi, 14ff.

11. Lawless, *Augustine*, esp. 55ff.

12. Lawless, *Augustine*, 45-58, but cf. P. Brown, *Augustine of Hippo, a Biography*, London 1972, 132-137.

13. K. Heussi, *Der Ursprung des Mönchtums*, reprint of 1936 edition, 1981; P. Nagel, *Die Motivierung der Askese in der alten Kirche und der Ursprung des Mönchtums*, *T.U.95*, Berlin 1966; *Dictionnaire de Spiritualité*, s.v. "monachisme"; J.C. O'Neill, "The Origins of Monasticism," in ed. R. Williams, *The Making of Orthodoxy. Essays in honour of Henry Chadwick*, Cambridge 1989, 270-287.

14. A. Guillaumont, "Monachisme et Ethique judéo-chrétienne" in *Rech. des Sciences Religieuses* LX (1972), 199-218; Shafiq Abouzayd, *Ihidayutha. A Study of the Life of Singleness in the Syrian Orient from Ignatius of Antioch to Chalcedon 451 A.D.*, Oxford 1993.

15. P. Brown, "The Rise and Function of the Holy Man in Late Antiquity," in *Society and the Holy in Late Antiquity*, London 1982, 103-152; *The Making of Late Antiquity*, Cambridge, MA, 1978, especially pp. 82-95. See also E.R. Dodds, *Pagan and Christian in an age of Anxiety: Some aspects of Religious experience from Marcus Aurelius to Constantine*, Cambridge 1965.

16. Brown, *Making*, 89. Brown argues that the authority of the Holy Man in the world of Late Antiquity was based on his separation from normal society which was no longer felt to have any available means of establishing contact with the Holy (cf. p. 11). Because the Holy Man had separated himself for this reason, he had a powerful social value for his fellow human beings.

17. *Ibid.*, 95; see also W.H.C. Frend, *Rise of Christianity*, London 1984, 422-423; 574-578.

18. See the work of P. Rousseau, for example in *Ascetics, Authority and the Church in the Age of Jerome and Cassian*, Oxford 1978; *Pachomius: the Making of a Community in Fourth Century Egypt*, Los Angeles 1985; Simon Tugwell's chapter on the Desert Fathers in *Ways of Imperfection*, London 1984, 13-24, is very helpful, and, most recently, Graham Gould, *The Desert Fathers on Monastic Community*, Oxford 1993.

19. Gould, *Desert Fathers*, 185.

20. *Ibid.*

21. For example, Cuthbert Butler, *Benedictine Monachism*, London 1924[2], repr. Cambridge 1961, 13. S. Tugwell's treatment of this issue should be noted, *Ways*, 19: "The austerities, whatever may have been their significance in earlier kinds of asceticism, are not viewed by the main tradition of the Egyptian desert as a way to become superhuman, nor as an ideal in themselves. They are very firmly subordinated to much more fundamental values such as humility and fraternal charity."

22. Thus R.A. Markus speaks of "City or Desert? Two models of Community," the title to chapter 11 of *End*, 157.

23. Barry Lopez, *Arctic Dreams*, London 1986, is an extraordinary study of the conventional idea of the desert, and of the hideous abuse of it as a result.

24. Tugwell, *Ways*, 14.

25. Cf. Tugwell, *Ways*, 17.

26. C. Peiffer, "The Biblical Foundations of Monasticism," in *CS 1* (1966), 7-31; D. Burton-Christie, *The Word in the Desert: Scripture and the Quest for Holiness in Early Christian Monasticism*, Oxford 1993.

27. Augustine, *De Doctrina Christiana*, Proem. 4ff.

28. DDC, IV Proem. 6.

29. Cf. Markus, *End*, 181ff, speaks of a blurring of frontiers between desert and city in the fifth century, thanks to people like Cassian, but the distinctions between Cassian and Augustine need not be so sharply drawn; see the review of his book in *Downside Review* 110 (1992) esp. pp. 71-74.

30. DDC, IV, with its rhetorical delineation of the Christian preacher, shows this particularly well, for example at iv, 6; for Christ as the wisdom of the Christian orator: v, 7 (referring to James 1:17), xxvii, 58 (quoting Phil. 1:18).

31. He adopts for this purpose the Platonist-inspired *enkyklios paideia*; see I. Hadot, *Arts libéraux et philosophie dans la pensée antique*, Paris 1984.

32. Augustine uses the picture of Moses spoiling the Egyptians, a patristic topos asserting that culture properly belongs to the Church, II, xl, 60, concluding the discussion of *artes liberales*, xix, 29ff.

33. Markus, *End*, 81, sees this very much as a distinguishing feature of Augustine's monasticism.

34. Augustine makes repeated use of the *locus classicus* of cenobitic monastic theology, Acts 4:32ff, but for the first time puts a special emphasis on the phrase *cor unum et anima una* by glossing it *in Deum*: Lawless, *Augustine*, 133.

35. Cf. Markus, *End*, 79-80; 175-176.

36. Nagel, *Motivierung*, 75-79; 105-107.

37. Augustine, *De Opere Monachorum*, xxv, 33. In general, see A. Zumkellar, *Das Moenchtum des heiligen Augustinus*, Würzburg 1968²; Eng. Transl.: *Augustine's Ideal of the Religious Life*, New York 1986, esp. pp. 188-199.

38. See especially Rosemarie Nürnberg, *Askese als sozialer Impuls: Monastisch-asketische Spiritualität als Wurzel und Triebfeder sozialer Ideen und Aktivitäten der Kirche in Südgallien im 5 Jahrhundert*, Bonn 1988.

39. Heussi, *Ursprung* 128, uses the term *Sonderwelt* to refer to the distinct environment which sets off the monastic life from normal society, cf. Markus, *End*, 67; but, *pace* Markus, p. 176, Augustine's ecclesiology still provides a theological way of distinguishing the monastic environment from the city.

40. *After Virtue*, London 1981, 245.

URBS MONASTICA:
FROM LOCUS TERRIBILIS
TO VISIO PACIS

Joël Letellier, OSB
(Abbaye Saint-Wandrille,
Caudebec en Caux, France)

Like an island in the city

During a recent discussion about monastic life with the novitiate of the Rouen monastery of the Benedictine nuns of the Blessed Sacrament, as we were considering the theme of the monastic city, a young sister began to develop the analogy that she saw—*mutatis mutandis*—between a monastery and the Ile de la Cité of Paris. This might seem surprising considering the tumultuous life of this large capital city and the almost ceaseless unfurling of crowds of tourists around Notre Dame. What a contrast with the peace, the silence, and the secluded life of a monastery.

Despite its obvious limitations, such a comparison can provide food for thought. Is the monastery not like a city within the great city of men? Is it not somewhat like the lungs that allow the great city to breathe fresh air, or like the heart which regularly and serenely pumps the life-giving stream that irrigates every part of the organism, or again like the memory that permits the soul to draw up from its deepest roots the best of all that God has given it and that preceding generations have handed on?

This whole spiritual and cultural heritage, which the waters of the Seine protect without fencing in, whose perimeter is clear but not restricted, thanks to the bridges that link the city of God to the present-day city of men, may serve as a metaphor for the monastic life.

It is noteworthy that the crossroads that gave birth to the place's economic life, the great meeting of the north-south and east-west axes of communication, was at the site of the modern Place du Châtelet, and that the spiritual cradle of the future Paris grew and gained strength at a slight distance from this center of commerce.

Gaulish ferrymen and farmers were the first to settle on the island when it was still marshy and inhospitable. It soon became a place of refuge and of worship for townsfolk. The sturdy nave of Notre Dame, close neighbor of the Sainte Chapelle and its precious relics, stands on the site of the pagan temple of Tiberius,[1] and of its successor, the Christian *ecclesia minor* mentioned by St. Gregory of Tours. Henceforth, this former marshy wilderness, transformed into a spiritual pole, would bear witness to the fact that a meeting of human roads would not amount to much were there not also for every man the meeting of his own road with God's.

Like a ship that forces its way through troubled waters, and that has weathered many narrow escapes from shipwreck, *fluctuat nec mergitur*[2]—Norman invasions, wars of religion, revolutionary troubles, world wars—the holy island with its precious heritage resembles those monasteries which, despite repeated threats and pillages, destructions and lootings, continue to bear witness to the constancy of heavenly realities, and hence of their superiority over all that is earthly. Even when in ruins, these houses of prayer continue to sing the praise of God, and if the monks return, the tempo of the monastic life resumes as though it had known no interruption.

Thus grew the Ile de la Cité, in step with God while remaining on the earth, and at the heart of the world, yet somewhat set apart, as though not being of this world, but already of the next.

Dare I add that if the array of human forces needed to accomplish such an artistic and intellectual exploit was extraordinary, as it was for each of our cathedrals, abbeys, and most beloved gems, and if we must be thankful to all the spiritual masters who raised up such monuments, as well as to all the architects and master craftsmen for all that they have left us, we must not fail to see the finger of God intervening in human history and giving his people sanctuaries and reliquaries to make known the beauty of heaven and able to draw down to earth blessings from on high: *"Nisi Dominus aedificaverit domum... Nisi*

Dominus custodierit civitatem…" (Ps. 126:1). That it is God who protects the city is surely the truth that Jean Fouquet wanted to depict in so evocative a way in his famous miniature in the fifteenth-century *Book of Hours of Etienne Chevalier,* in which the hand of God appears in the sky above Paris, over the cathedral, and blesses the city at the hour of Vespers.[3]

Maurice de Sully, although a great builder and man of God, was the Bishop of Paris, and not the abbot of a monastery. He built a cathedral, not an abbey church, and the Ile de la Cité was never an *Urbs monastica.* However, it is important to remember that the year 1160 saw the beginning of a new period of architectural creation. The Bishop of Paris could not remain indifferent to monastic constructions like the nearby, and still new, abbey church of Saint-Denis, the masterpiece of Abbot Suger.[4] There can be no doubt but that such a church had a decisive influence upon the construction of several cathedrals, particularly those of Senlis, Noyon and Laon. As well, had not the famous abbot of Saint-Denis given a splendid stained-glass window to the old church of Notre Dame en l'Ile, which from 1190 until the eighteenth century, found its home in the new cathedral?

The relationship of Maurice de Sully with the monks of Saint Germain-des-Prés was not so happy, for the consecration of the choir of the new church of this abbey, which was destined for great fame in a later age, took place in the same year as the laying of the foundation stone of the cathedral. On April 21, 1163, the day of the consecration by Pope Alexander III, Maurice de Sully arrived for the ceremony. However, the monks asked him to leave, since they feared that the presence of the Bishop of Paris might imply that they were in some way his subjects. It is easy to imagine both the unfortunate prelate's return to his cathedral, and the thoughts he was turning over in his mind. He must have sighed, *"Terribilis locus iste, hic est domus monachorum."* To calm himself, he may have called to mind the fable of the bird of paradise that he himself had written for his people with great success. He may have thought of the blessed monk of the legend, caught up in ecstasy for three hundred years, charmed by the song of a bird, a comforting *visio pacis,* after all.

Thus do men build and dedicate upon earth sanctuaries for the God of heaven.

Like a city in the desert

Derwas Chitty entitled his well-known book describing the origins of Egyptian and Palestinian monasticism *The Desert a City*. First published in English in 1966, it appeared in French in 1980, several years after its author's premature death, with a title that is even more explicit: *Et le desert devint une cité (And the Desert Became a City).*[5] There is nothing original in the expression; the author took it from chapter fourteen of the famous *Life of Antony* by Athanasius, which tells how the great ascetic set out to convince many others to live a life of solitude. Thus, the *Vita Antonii* tells how dwellings appeared on the mountains. The desert was soon filled with monks—"*et desertum repletum est monachis,*" according to the Latin manuscripts—those men who have abandoned their homes to embrace a heavenly way of life— "*et professi sunt caelestem conversationem.*" The two canals of the Latin tradition—the anonymous translation, discovered by A. Wilmart, and the better-known translation by Evagrius of Antioch—express imperfectly the Greek term used by Athanasius. *Epolisthè*, containing the word "city," permits the author, by the juxtaposition of the two antagonistic terms *"Hè érèmos épolisthè,"* to establish with one stroke of the pen both the extent of the new-born monasticism and the paradox that it embodies.[6]

At first, it was only a question of anchorites who, already numerous, and still rapidly increasing in number, were spread out in several different clusters. Beset on all sides, Antony could no longer live at Pispir. In 312, he set out for Mount Qolzoum, his "interior mountain." In a few years, an astounding people athirst for God spread out in the desert of Lower Egypt; the names of the famous groups of Nitria, the Cells and Scetis are inseparably linked with those of Antony, Amoun and Macarius the Egyptian. Around 373, Rufinus, in his *Ecclesiastical History*, estimated that the semi-anchoritic monks of Nitria counted at least three thousand men, and twenty years later, Palladius thought that they numbered five thousand, distributed amongst about fifty residences *(monai)*, housing from two or three monks to more than two hundred.

In 338, Nitria was already so heavily populated that it had become essential that certain monks be permitted to go out further into the desert in order to live a life of greater solitude. The famous walk of Amoun, along with Antony, then 87 years old, lay at the origin of the Cells, a sort of isolated annex about ten miles away from Nitria. Six hundred anchorites soon came to inhabit this solitude, each in his own cell, a *monasterium* built of clay bricks, set in a small garden. Their great number, and their isolation from one other, since each had to be out of earshot of his neighbors, caused the Cells to cover a vast area, more than ten kilometers around.

The archaeological excavations carried out in 1964 under the direction of Antoine Guillaumont, who declared that he had found himself in the presence of the remains of "a veritable monastic city,"[7] have confirmed what Palladius tells in the *Lausiac History*, as well as the narrative of the Palestinian monks who visited the Cells in 394-395, a narrative which Rufinus adapted and translated into Latin in his *Historia Monachorum in Aegypto*. Rufinus himself had firsthand knowledge of the Cells, having visited the place in 374.

Although the desert of Scetis was relatively less populated than Nitria, because of its greater isolation, as well as because of its being more exposed to barbarian incursions, it seems that this desert counted about three thousand monks in the mid-sixth century, after the difficult period of relaxation of discipline, increasing emigration to Palestine, and a temporary interruption at the beginning of the fifth century, following the raids of the barbarian Mazices.

Alongside the impressive monastic implantations of Lower Egypt, it is important to remember the birth and development of cenobitic Pachomian monasticism, which began in Tabennesi in Upper Egypt when it was but an abandoned village. One day, the young Pachomius heard a voice saying, "Stay here and build a monastery, for many will come to you to become monks." After his master Palamon had assured him that the voice was indeed divine, he build a hut at the place where he had heard the voice. A few years later, when the large monastery that replaced it had become insufficient, he founded the cenobium of Phbow three kilometers away; afterwards, many other monasteries were founded, or affiliated themselves to a great congregation of monastic communities. Eleven appeared during Pachomius' lifetime; by the sixth century there would be twenty-four. Tabennesi soon counted 1,300 monks, as did Phbow. According to Cassian, when Pachomius died in May 346, his disciples numbered three if not five thousand monks. A few years later, Palladius, followed by Sozomen, would speak of seven thousand monks. Jerome's figure of 50,000 seems "to belong to the realm of fantasy," to quote Jean-Claude Guy.[8]

Nonetheless, taking into consideration the whole of the monastic population of Upper and of Lower Egypt, including Shenoute's strict monastery known as the White Convent, the monks of Oxyrhynchus, who were as numerous as the inhabitants of the city, and the six hundred or so monasteries around Alexandria, a figure of 500,000 monks for fifth-century Egypt would not seem to be exaggerated. There is no need to look any further to justify calling the whole country an *Urbs monastica*.[9]

It is of course out of the question to review all of monastic history, region by region, period by period, or to make a statistical inquiry into the fluctuations of the number of monks over the ages, but it is important to notice that in this first vigorous growth of monasticism on Egyptian soil, there appears with a great deal of variety and a certain number of astonishing contrasts the very thing that will manifest itself and develop throughout the course of history, wherever monasticism is implanted. This is by no means to maintain that in the first generations of Egyptian monasticism everything is said, and that no innovation or new monastic adaptation with any claim to legitimacy saw or ever will see the light of day anywhere else. It would be a clumsy falsification of history to refuse to take into account the noteworthy differences in the conception, organization and realization of monastic life according to various ages, regions, mentalities, political and economic contexts, and in general everything that may have influenced the development of the monastic phenomenon over the centuries, from within as well as from without.

An incontestable fact stands out through all monastic history: whenever men go out into solitude to seek God with all their heart, others follow and join them, so that the greatly desired

solitude always finds itself menaced. A minimum of organization and elementary precautions has thus proved itself to be
indispensable, from the spiritual as well as from the material
point of view. The chosen place, desert or marsh, mountain or
thick forest, is rapidly transformed from an inhospitable waste
into fertile land, a green oasis, a populated site, and almost
always a source of civilization.

With the exception of the few isolated hermits who, shelter-
ing in a cave, a cabin or some rudimentary construction, man-
aged to keep their retreat a secret, one cannot but notice that
wherever monks appear, so do extensive buildings. Of course,
these are necessary for the cenobitic life, but they often became
vital as protection against all sorts of undesirable incursions,
from prowling animals to looting brigands to persecuting troops.
The modest walls which served to indicate in a symbolic way the
spiritual cloister sometimes became veritable ramparts, and it
is not rare to see monasteries resembling fortresses, castles
equipped with a keep and even a drawbridge.

Such fortifications have at times proved most efficacious, but
in general they afforded only a limited degree of protection.
Without running to such defenses, a great number of monasteries are impressive because of their vastness, architecture, lands
or industry; that is to say, impressive by the whole of the
dynamic life not only lived within the enclosure, but also
spreading to the outside world through a web of spiritual,
economic, social, cultural and political relationships.

Hence the essential contrast to be borne in mind, and which is
true of nearly every age: the monk wanted to flee the city and the
world by retiring to the desert, but, paradoxically, he dwells in a
veritable city, and becomes a craftsman within a great harmoni-
ous assembly which at once serves and constrains him, of which
he is not the master, and which might even absorb him entirely.
The original *locus terribilis*, inhospitable, but greatly desired, has
given place to the *urbs monastica*, capable of ennobling the land
and of refining souls. A city that is always industrious and full of
life, in some cases unobtrusive, in others imposing, determined
to find her joy in God, unable to withdraw from this world, to
which she physically belongs, although already living in the
next, it wishes to be, and indeed is, that privileged place to which

these well-known words of St. Jerome can be attributed: *"O desertum Christi floribus vernans! O solitudo, in qua illi nascuntur lapides, de quibus in Apocalypsi civitas magni regis extruitur! O heremus familiari Deo gaudens!"*[10]

The city of letters, arts and sciences

The Word of God, Holy Scripture, that library which the Bible constitutes, is the food with which monks have never ceased to nourish themselves since they first appeared. This Word of God, heard, read, meditated, ruminated, memorized and put into practice, accompanies the true monk without interruption. St. Antony already exhorted his disciples to conform themselves to the divine commandments, and to write them in their hearts without letting a single divine word fall upon the ground through their own negligence. The Rule of St. Pachomius obliges all those who enter the community to learn to read, and to memorize long passages of Scripture. St. Theodore, Pachomius' favorite disciple and his successor after Horsiesius, is known as well to have had the habit of gathering a great number of the brethren under a palm tree where he would teach them and, following the example of Pachomius, would give each of them a different divine word before dismissing them. Each brother carried this word away with him like a precious treasure which he must not loose whatever happens.[11]

From the earliest times of monasticism until our own day, monks have always desired to build their spiritual life on the foundation of *lectio divina*, an assiduous, meditative and prayerful reading of the *pagina sacra*, which imparts to them God's very thought by means of his Word. On the basis of the heritage of Origen, Evagrius and Cassian, St. Basil and St. Benedict, those great legislators of East and West, urged their monks always to remain faithful to its practice. Who could claim to measure the influence that St. Jerome, St. Augustine and St. Gregory the Great have exercised in this sphere? The mere names of all those great monks who have commented, sung and lived the Word of God, including Caesarius of Arles, the Venerable Bede, Rabanus Maurus, Anselm of Bec, Pierre de Celle and John of Fécamp, suffice to illuminate the treasures of Scripture. They were so familiar with the sacred text that all their writings are woven with biblical reminiscences. Then there is St. Bernard, the unsurpassed troubadour of the Scriptures. The famous names of William of Saint-Thierry, Guerric of Igny, Aelred of Rievaulx and Isaac of Stella come to mind, along with others like Guigo II the Carthusian, whose *Ladder for Monks* contains a famous passage which summarizes the teaching he had received from monastic tradition and that Hugh of Saint-Victor had recently codified, outlining the well-known *cursus* of the monk who, beginning with *lectio*, continues on his way towards *meditatio, oratio* and *contemplatio*.

To tell the truth, the holy books carefully replaced in the *armarium claustri* after each liturgical or private reading, and unfailingly recopied century after century by an unbroken chain of scribes in the best scriptoria, were not the only books to be held in reverence and cared for attentively. Holy Scripture was as it were crowned by the great commentaries that set off its qualities. This imposing and varied *bibliotheca sanctorum Patrum*, to use the phrase which a sixteenth-century precursor of the Maurists, the learned Marguerin de la Bigne, canon of Bayeux, used as the title of his editorial achievement, was considerably augmented with the passage of time by a precious inheritance coming from the best Latin and Greek sources, the spiritual and cultural capital which each generation of monks received, enriched, and handed on in turn to its successors.

If a copyist took a good year at least to transcribe the whole Bible, a medium-sized manuscript required two or three months. Needs were great. The monks set out to satisfy their piety and to quicken their intellect and, in so doing, they rescued the learning of classical antiquity. The whole inestimable treasure of classical literature, pagan and Christian, was saved from extinction and has come down to us by way of the quill of our monk-scribes. For the Carolingian period alone, more than eight thousand manuscripts recopied in cloisters still exist today. Cicero, Virgil and Tacitus were preserved thanks to Carolingian scriptoria. How many authors were sought out, copied, and safeguarded for the future! According to the vicissitudes of circumstances, times and tastes, Ovid, Horace, Suetonius, Quintillian and other classical authors rub shoulders with the Fathers of the Church. Phaedrus and Terence are recopied between St. Basil and St. Augustine,

Plautinus and Juvenal with St. Gregory and St. Ephrem. The list of the principal scriptoria is endless; besides, their activity peaked at different moments. The most famous names include Luxeuil and Corbie, Fleury and Saint-Denis, Saint Martin of Tours and Saint-Amand, Saint-Gall, Reichenau and Fulda, Bobbio and Monte Cassino, Winchester and Canterbury, and of course Cluny and Clairvaux.

Monks have always loved the Bible, holy learning, and as a result came to love learning in general, those studies which broaden the mind and the soul as they impart knowledge. Two great figures in this domain have yet to be named, two personalities who together suffice to evoke a whole context, a complete state of mind: Cassiodorus at Vivarium and Mabillon at Saint Germain-des-Prés. From sixth-century Calabria to seventeenth-century Paris, there is a striking continuity in the love of learning. In the twelfth century, Geoffroy of Breteuil, prior of Sainte-Barbe in Neustria, liked to say that a monastery without books was like a fortress without munitions: *Claustrum sine armario, Quasi castrum sine armamentario.*[12]

This well-turned phrase has been handed on to posterity; this is why monks have always cared for their library and, with certain rare and unfortunate exceptions, have always sought to swell its holdings, even when times were hard. At the same time as it reflects the vitality of an abbey, the library, along with the studies that it fosters, is also the source of a spiritual life more surely founded upon the solidity of the Tradition of the Church and upon the world of knowledge in general. This is one of the most sure and most necessary foundations of the *Urbs monastica: fides exauditu.*

Two essential links in the chain of the transmission of knowledge and faith were thus formed by the claustral schools and the copyists' workshops. However, their activities do not represent the sum total of the work carried out within a monastery.[13] This microcosm, a well-regulated and ordered city, exists above all for prayer and for the praise of God. Although this activity occupies the first place in the life of the monk as in the life of the community, it by no means excludes other occupations, responsibilities and crafts. A multitude of varied talents and skills, along with tried and true methods, helped to meet the needs of tens, sometimes hundreds of brothers, allowed them to succor the poor of the neighborhood, and even, as was often the case, brought to the outside world all that only a stable and permanent structure, rich in knowledge and capability, could hand on and teach.

No historian can fail to acknowledge the powerful civilizing role that monasteries played for centuries, particularly during certain crucial periods between the collapse of the ancient world and the slow creation of a new society. The monasteries were invariably homes of intense intellectual, artistic and spiritual culture, and centers of diffusion of the most solid moral values. They acted as powerful levers in economic, agricultural, and industrial development, not merely in a few areas but throughout Europe. Since the same sap flowed in all the branches of the monastic order, and since these branches spread to cover all of Christendom, the principle of capillary attraction was reinforced by the strength that lies in numbers. The abbeys, linked together by bonds of filiation or by other groupings, which allowed each house to preserve its own characteristics and a degree of autonomy which varied according to the circumstances, constituted an immense backdrop, criss-crossed all of Christendom, and established frontier posts on the boundaries of lands that had not yet heard the Gospel. The considerable missionary activity that monks have carried out in varying manners should never be forgotten. The names of Gregory the Great, Augustine of Canterbury, Boniface, Willibrord and Ansgar symbolize this dimension of monasticism.

In every monastery, from the least to the greatest, there was the same rhythm, regulated by the succession of prayer, study and work, the same ideal of holiness, the same search for solitude and silence, the same influence upon the world outside, although in proportion to the size of the community and in accordance with local circumstances. The same occupations, the same general arrangement of the buildings, the same family spirit could be found everywhere, albeit with an infinite diversity and an astonishing adaptability. It is incontestable that all this was so for the most part thanks to the continuing active influence upon material and juridicial organization of the genius of Rome, sharpened by the spirit of the Gospel, and tempered by

Benedictine discretion. Was not even the layout of the monastery
the direct descendant of the Roman villa, with the atrium in the
middle and, around the porticoes, the buildings in which the
familia lived, particularly the *triclinium* or dining room and the
exedrium or common room, along with the bedchambers and
many other rooms? Besides all this, there were also the farm
buildings with various workshops and other dependencies. Thus
there are relatively few differences between the layout of an
ancient Roman house, as described by Vitruvius and Palladio, or
revealed by archaeological excavations, and our monasteries of
yesterday and today. Many new elements have made their
appearance—first of all, the church—but the primitive plan has
scarcely changed. Besides this physical borrowing from the
Roman world, which manifests itself in a desire for order, preci-
sion and functional efficiency at the same time as for well-being,
intimacy and beauty, there are also elements borrowed from the
realm of juridicial organization. This organization, in the West,
was permeated by the Latin spirit and laid down by St. Benedict
in his admirable *Regula monachorum*, demanding, yet characterized by lightness of touch, relatively short, but rich in experience
and full of wisdom. Even today the full extent of its capacity to
burgeon out into new life has yet to be measured.[14]

One of the essential strengths of the Rule lies in its requirement of stability. St. Benedict is even more firm than St. Basil
in his desire to exclude the disastrous consequences of the way
of life of the gyrovagues. A Benedictine monk's first vow is
of stability in his monastery,[15] which attaches him definitively to
a household, to the brethren, to an abbot. Of course, obedience
may require him to go out of the monastery, although such
absences are rare, or it may send him to another community, for
example, to a foundation, or in order to help out elsewhere, but
such departures are exceptional. The principle of stability roots
a monk in his monastery, fosters a genuine family spirit in
a shared *amor loci*, and places him unambiguously under the
authority of his abbot, making him his disciple and true spiritual
son.

The important spiritual advantages that the practice of stability brings lead St. Benedict to require that the monastery contain
everything that is necessary to permit the monks to avoid useless

and even harmful trips outside. In the chapter concerning the porters, he says:

> The monastery should, if possible, be so arranged that all necessary things *(omnia necessaria)*, such as water, mill, garden and various crafts may be within the enclosure *(intra monasterium)*, so that the monks may not be compelled to wander outside it *(vagandi foras)*, for that is not at all expedient for their souls *(omnino non expedit animabus eorum).*[16]

Dom Delatte remarks in his Commentary on the Rule:

> Thus, a complete monastery resembles a small city. This was the case of many monasteries of the Thebaid, where each group of craftsmen dwelt in its own district. In the West, after St. Benedict, certain great abbeys were organized in an admirable manner and comprised an even greater variety of artisans and artists.[17]

In the days of St. Antony, the manual work of the anchorites consisted mainly of braiding ropes and making mats, baskets and sandals with willow and palm leaves. At Nitria, besides the church and a guest house, there was a bursary and no fewer than seven bakehouses, for the monks of the Cells depended on Nitria for their bread. At the Cells, as in the Pachomian *koinonia*, the weaving of linen developed. At Phbow, there was a workshop with room for twenty-two weavers. Manual work was so important and so well organized in these monasteries of Upper Egypt that they sometimes give the impression of having been veritable factories.

In point of fact, as soon as monks put in their appearance, they exploit all the possibilities of the land, make it bear fruit, and never fail to turn to advantage the varying conditions in which they find themselves. In the desert, they create oases; in forests, which are the deserts of temperate regions, they clear land and cultivate it, thus creating arable land and considerably increasing its extent. Lands brought into cultivation in this way were known as *novalia*. According to the nature of the soil and the geographical situation, the monks cultivated grains, planted market gardens, created orchards, or practiced stock farming. In certain areas, they covered the land with vineyards, not only in

Burgundy at Clos-Vougeot, for example, but even near Paris, as did Abbot Suger when he finished clearing the forest of Vaucresson, which until then had been a haunt of thieves.

Here, monks create mill-races, install dams, divert a river, catch and sell fish; there, they become smiths, fullers, metal-founders, masons, carpenters, joiners. All the trades are represented, and each monk-craftsman has his workshop, his range of activities, his proficiency. According to the circumstances, he might receive help from other brothers or, following a decision of the abbot or the cellarer in charge of the estate, change his activity and serve elsewhere. Sometimes a number of laymen, more or less attached to the monastery, living in its shadow and under the crozier, swell the total population of the monastery and increase the productivity of the farm, the industries or the commerce. This body of lay helpers soon became indispensable in the greater houses, and sometimes counted a considerable number of members.

Temporal well-being may of course give a more solid material base to an abbey's spiritual influence, but too great a degree of material prosperity has often paradoxically endangered or even helped to destroy the true monastic spirit of a community or a congregation. Monastic history is full of examples of the sorry consequences that such softening inevitably brings. But this dark side of the matter apart, no one can deny the powerful role in economic and social development that the great abbeys, centers of agricultural, industrial and commercial life, played, along with, above and beyond the individual monasteries, the great network of the abbeys taken together, each one in its own particular context.

Art is situated at the limit of the material and spiritual worlds. It is rooted in matter, is formed of matter, but is constituted by the most noble of man's spiritual aspirations, and nourishes him more than any earthly food. It comprises architecture and illuminations, jewelry and Gregorian chant, painting and sculpture, ranges from the sumptuous to the austere, yet remains eloquent, proceeding from the heart of monks caught up by their meeting with the infinite.[18] It is impossible to describe or even simply to list here the different and varied forms of monastic art, but this fundamental aspect of monastic life cannot be passed over in silence; how many tourists in our own time have been struck by this art as they take "the tour of the abbeys." The sum of the treasures left by the monks of bygone days, scattered about the countryside and at the heart of cities, or collected in museums and books, is vast. There are surviving monuments or, as at Cluny, their memory. There is the "marvel" of Mont Saint-Michel, and there are humbler monasteries like Le Thoronet and Sénanque. Here, little priories hide in woods, marshes or valleys, and there they dominate a plateau—*Bernardus valles, montes Benedictus amabat*. Still others perch like an eagle's nest half-way up a rocky escarpment, as at Saint Martin-du-Canigou. The praise of God and all the other activities of monastic life continue in living abbeys, while others, whose missing elements are either irretrievably lost or, like the cloisters of Montrejeau and Saint Michel-de-Cuxa, are in "safekeeping" in the Bahamas or Manhattan, lie in ruins. There is something that proceeds from this assembled treasury which is unique, even incomprehensible, which calls forth admiration, gratitude and prayer.

For it was in prayer that all this was built, that the ribs of the vaulting and the stones were designed, hewn and assembled, that the chalices, shrines, reliquaries and books inlaid with ivory were created, that the technique of illumination and of miniatures was developed, and that wall painting, particularly from the ninth century, began to tell the story of the Bible. It was in the same atmosphere of prayer, as well as to arouse and intensify it, that, already in the late tenth century, particularly in the abbeys of St. Emmeram of Ratisbon, and of Tegernsee in Bavaria, and above all in the eleventh and twelfth centuries, the master glass makers showed the extent of their talents. Every monastery had its artistic school because engraving metal, like pouring glass or dressing stone, are all different ways of praising the Creator of all things. Let it suffice to think of the famous treasury of Sainte-Foy de Conques, in particular the splendid figure in majesty sculpted in yew, covered with gold leaf, set with enamels and precious stones, a masterpiece of this monastery's tenth-century goldsmith's workshop. Art is an expression of faith, but it gives rise to faith as well. Simply to gaze at Fontenay or Noirlac, Vezelay or Moissac, is enough to understand that the art that proceeds from contemplation is also the most beautiful apostolate. "Our spirit is so weak," said Abbot Suger, "that it is only through the realities that the senses perceive that it can rise up to heaven."

The art of music is one of these realities that exalt the spirit. Gregorian chant, the contemporary of all this monastic development over the centuries, was and remains one of the most perfect forms of spiritual art. Monks were perhaps not all cantors, just as they were not all sculptors, glaziers, calligraphers or painters of miniatures, but all knew and loved these melodies that formed their heart and soul by opening them day after day to the understanding of realities on high:

> *Lapides pretiosi omnes muri tui,*
> *et turres Jerusalem gemmis aedificabuntur...*[19]
> *Surge et illuminare Jerusalem:*
> *quia gloria Domini super te orta est.*[20]

Like a desert in the city

Like many other anchorites, Arsenius, who had looked for solitude in the desert of Scetis, found himself hard pressed on all sides. The isolated spot he had chosen became a city inhabited by monks, so he decided to take himself further away, just as the great Antony had done earlier. Arsenius had abandoned the imperial court of Constantinople, where he had been an important official, yet he found himself mixed up in the *politeia* of the monks of Scetis. When Abba Mark asked him, "Why do you run away from us?" Arsenius, an old man, answered, "God knows I love you, but I cannot be with both God and men."[21] For Arsenius, the call of the desert was radical, and this attraction for solitude was by no means romantic or illusory. The desert had already shown him its ambivalence, being on the one hand the terrible place of thirst, dryness and isolation, the place of wild beasts, brigands and outcasts, the place of phantasms and temptations, suffering and death, in a word, the place of demons, and hence the perfect site for spiritual combat; yet on the other hand, and as a result of these, it is also the place where purification and unification become possible, the place of victory over enemy forces, the place of *hesychia* and perhaps of the eagerly sought *apatheia*, the place which God chose in times past to conclude his

Covenant with his people, the place which can also be the setting for the engagement and the encounter, for friendship and closeness with God.

This notion of the desert, rich in contrasts and of biblical origin, is clearly much more realistic than those of Hellenistic philosophy and of the mysticism of Philo, even though the latter is strongly influenced, not to say permeated, by the Bible. Both currents minimize the importance of the struggle which the spiritual combat of the desert requires, and consider only the idealistic and purely contemplative aspect of life hidden away from the worry of business and the disorderliness of cities, a vision which is overly idyllic and not a little romanticized.[22]

The divine call heard under some form or other, the invitation to abandon everything in order to give oneself up to the search for God alone, lies at the origin of the monastic vocation. In order to answer this interior call, the monk, henceforth fascinated by the realities on high, begins to divest himself of everything that could hamper his spiritual quest. From the very start, he understands that he can be the Lord's true disciple only if he gives up his possessions and his self-will. This indispensable renunciation, which Our Lord himself announced, in particular in Luke 14:33, "None of you can be my disciple without giving up all that he owns," even lent itself as a name for the earliest monks. Before being a *monachos*, the ascetic was first, and more fundamentally, an *apotaktikos:* one who renounces. Pachomius is referred to thus in the *Coptic Lives.* The same word was used in Egypt during the first centuries of monasticism to designate the anchorite who had given up his possessions in order to withdraw to the desert.[23]

Such a renunciation of self and of possessions should not only characterize the dawn of monastic life, but also constitute its very essence in its individual and collective aspects. In this way, monastic life is resolutely placed in relation to Christ, who freely emptied himself by accomplishing for us the great sacraments of his Incarnation and his Paschal Mystery. It is only in this *sequela Christi,* which each member of a monastic community lives out mysteriously and intensely, that the foundation and the reality of the *Urbs monastica,* city of God, can be uncovered and understood.

The entire course of personal conversion is evidently at issue here. If the monk does not descend into the *locus terribilis* of his heart and his will to clear out the evil tendencies and purify the soil there, in order to give himself up to the demanding exercises of the spiritual art and to ready himself against any lying invasion, he will never be able to contemplate the *visio pacis* of a soul that the Lord has made new.

Here is the heart of every monastic city, beyond the visible city, beyond the source of civilization or economic power, beyond the source of literature or polished art. The real monastic city is incontestably the heart of each monk, transformed by the divine sculptor, who is at once gardener, architect, painter and doctor. In his Rule, St. Benedict lists the tools of the spiritual craft, the famous *instrumenta artis spiritalis*,[24] which alone can build in each soul what God wills, an outline of the heavenly Jerusalem.

Wherever he may be, even—or rather, above all—at the heart of a numerous monastic community, the monk should often withdraw into his interior mountain or to some uninhabited place to find himself *solus cum Deo*, by no means in order to run away from his responsibilities towards his brethren, but rather to fertilize the soil of his heart, the better to serve them. The monk's duty is to put his own way of thinking in harmony with that of the God whom he wishes to serve, following the example of St. Benedict, who felt the need to enter into himself or, as his biographer, St. Gregory, puts it, *"habitavit secum."* By renouncing his self-will—without any sort of running away whatsoever—the monk who obeys by love the order he has received, however hard and restricting it may be, can be led to find himself configured in truth, if mysteriously, to the great mystery of the death and resurrection of Christ. The veritable desert is there, a land of aridity and thirst, but at the same time the terrible land of communication without guile. Within the sanctuary of his heart, the monk then experiences that Paschal Mystery which allows him to pass over from the *locus terribilis* to the *visio pacis*.

If a monk's obedience to his abbot must be unconditional, the abbot's government is anything but arbitrary. St. Benedict does not stint in the recommendations of prudence, wisdom and compassion for human affliction which he makes to the man who occupies the place of Christ in the monastery. Here St. Benedict shows an acute sense of God and his demands, at the same time as a concrete realism, characterized by humanity and by a profound respect for the brothers. The one cannot do without the other, for the human relationships among the members of a community must be ordered in the light of the *agape* of God. The opposite of a utopia—all the attempted constructions of which in the course of history have ended in dramatic failures—the monastic society, founded on the gift of self rather than on the desire for power and possessions, upon the spirit of service and the free response to the divine impulse, has provided abundant and eloquent examples over the ages of genuine *koinonia* founded upon the spirit of sacrifice and love, in a great and genuine mutual respect and in a constant search for the things that please God.

The spirit of St. John the Baptist should quicken all the members of the monastic community. Following the example of the Precursor, they must leave for the desert and remain available, accomplish their mission, and then stand aside when the Lord approaches, for it is He who must increase and act. They must make over their souls entirely to him, then withdraw into the shade, and die to the world. This is the monk's humble and noble service, the ground plan of every authentic spiritual life. The servant cannot be greater than his master. Now the Master himself has taken the road to the *locus terribilis* of the laceration of death, passing through the dreadful place of burial. "There is no love greater than to give one's life for one's friends."

It is thus possible to arrive at one of the fairest fruits of this mutual gift of self within a monastic community. In Chapter 72 of his Rule, undoubtedly one of its summits, St. Benedict describes it, for he shows how the *zelus amaritudinis malus* disappears to make way for the *zelus bonus*, founded upon humility and charity. St. Dorotheus of Gaza gives a beautiful description of what the unity of a monastery should be, a unity created by the diversity of its members, joined together by the bond of charity and peace:

> What are monasteries, in your opinion? Are they not like one body with its members?... Are you the head? Then

govern. Are you the eye? Be attentive and watch. Are you the mouth? Speak with good purpose. Are you the ear? Obey. The hand? Work. The foot? Accomplish your task. Let each one work for the body according to his abilities. Always be eager to help each other, by teaching and sowing the Word of God in your brother's heart, by consoling him in time of trial, or by coming to his aid and helping him with his work. In a word, take care to be united to one another, as I have said, each one according to his abilities. For the more each one is united to his neighbor, the more he is united to God.[25]

And Dorotheus continues with the well-known example of the circle with rays, an eloquent image which many spiritual masters have repeated since the sixth century.

Happily, there have been and still are many monks able to sing the couplet: *"Ecce quam bonum et quam jucundum habitare fratres in unum!"* The monastery may indeed seem to be a splendid work of art or a model of organization, but it is above all a privileged place where souls enamored of God devote themselves to the difficult spiritual art of renunciation and interior deprivation. It is because the monk submits himself to his abbot that he carries out some task or other; because he remains open to the workings of grace that he experiences a strange liberation; because he gives himself unreservedly to his brothers that he receives everything from them; and it is because he hands himself over to the hard spiritual combat of the desert that he becomes a cause of peace in the midst of his brethren.

> *O quam metuendus est locus iste!*
> *Vere non est hic aliud nisi domus Dei et porta caeli.*[26]

Paradox and communion

Sheltered from big cities with their agitation and tumult, monasteries appear to be a sort of protected reserve where the remarkable and seemingly fossilized remains of a distant past are conserved and where rare species on the road to extinction can survive for a few more decades. Monks, along with their monuments, ancestral customs and green environment, have plenty of elements to interest those who devote themselves lovingly to the precious inheritance of a civilization which, alas, is becoming more and more generally forgetful of its roots and its first movements. Romantics, nostalgic for the past, film-makers searching for medieval backdrops, ecologists and psychosociologists of religious phenomena can certainly find pasture there for a while but, for my part, I prefer historians, archaeologists and archivists, as well as those who protect, defend and classify. They have hard labor and a noble task to accomplish, fraught with difficulties, but rich in promise and joy. However, cloisters are not destined for them in the first place either; they remain religious buildings above all, which men of prayer have built and organized, which prayer has thought out and inhabited, and which, by the intermediary of tangible materials and symbolic forms, speak to souls in love with spiritual realities.

The spiritual art, if it is fully accomplished and complete (something that happens but rarely, and then only in a soul of outstanding sanctity), is by its nature timeless and universal. Thus it bears the characteristic mark of human nature as well as the mark of the divine nature. The two natures, without confusion or mixture but in harmony with one another, reach out into each other's hidden depths, and build the only possible bridge between our sublunary world and the world on high, reconciling the ephemeral particular with the eternal universal.

The true cloister is the heart of a Christian, and the only true and perfect cloister, bearing within it the fullness of the images of both heaven and earth, was achieved once in the person of Christ. Other cloisters of flesh or of stone are but reflections, intermediaries, echoes. Is not Our Lady the most beautiful of all creatures, shining with native beauty, a pure reflection of the beauty and holiness of God? She is *hortus conclusus, fons signatus* and *porta caeli* all at once. She is the masterpiece of the spiritual art perfectly carved by the divine sculptor, the monastic city fitted above all others to receive in her womb the creating and recreating Word, and who, bringing this Word into the world, never ceased to keep him intact in her heart.

Matter irrigated by the spiritual soul evokes the higher dimension to which grace never ceases to call man. Whether an interior sanctuary or a microcosm of the regenerated universe, the cloister and its neighboring church, at the heart of the monastery, symbolize paradise regained, not so much the paradise lost in the past as the paradise to be realized in the future, prefigured by the symbolism of numbers, space and iconography, and in a way anticipated by the rhythm of the conventual life, fraternal communion and the radiant interplay of sacramental signs. If the *paradisus claustralis* is the architectural center of the monastic city, the sanctuary of the church is the heart on the liturgical and sacramental plane. A mysterious correspondence has grown up between the well and the altar, the depth and the height, between the quadrangle of the cloisters and the transept crossing, which takes into account the orientation of the church and the resulting play of light, a sense of proportion, appropriate forms, the choice of materials and the ornamentation. Everything is regulated, measured and decided with a multitude of mathematical as well as scriptural resonances. Nonetheless, a healthy and genuine freedom of expression plays its part, the freedom of God's children, a notion dear to the sons of St. Benedict, a freedom which, while remaining in the uprightness of faith and using technical know-how, understands how to reconcile the tradition handed on by the elders with a spirit of innovation and creativity, a spirit which God himself undoubtedly inspired in the hearts of monk-architects and master craftsmen.

Like a reliquary, the monastery constitutes an *imago mundi*, not a scale model of the universe containing in miniature all the tensions inherent in the cosmos, but a microcosm which, although physically reduced and geographically circumscribed, nonetheless encompasses the sum of the forces of the universe in full strength, powers which sometimes oppose each other, both converging and antagonistic tensions, as well as weaknesses and wounds.

Situated at the crossroads of matter and spirit, of time and eternity, the cloister, like the altar, while belonging to this world, already attains the next. The human heart, eager to find God, establishes itself in its *peregrinatio Dei* in this odd place made for man and for God, made by man and by God, set apart from the world and yet the very center of the world, wherein both the mystery of the cosmos and the mystery of humanity are reflected in a way that is both mysterious and awe-inspiring, by way of numerous profound correspondences. The man who lives within this sacred enclosure experiences in his flesh the wounds that the world suffers, just as the temple built of stones also proclaims this tragedy and bears it in its architecture, its symbolic imagery and its sacramental ordering. The cross, touching the four cardinal points, rooted in the earth through its crypt, and rising up to the heights of the heavens, proclaims that distances and antagonisms cannot prevail over the forces of communion and life. Life gushes out in an incomprehensible movement—*vita in motu*. Its source is the same altar, the same crossroads; it comes with the light of the rising sun—*sol invictus*—and, *via salutis*, is present in the baptismal font and the symbol of the octagon, a reminder that henceforth the re-creation of man in the redemption wrought by Christ is still more extraordinary than was the beauty of the universe in the beginning.

Like the monk, the cloister displays this new consecration of the entire universe, where the hostile powers, still at large, are nonetheless already vanquished, and where the first fruits of peace have become sufficiently abundant and enduring as to leave no doubt that recovery is on its way. The universe suffers because it has been separated from God for too long, but alas, it does not yet understand, or does not want to understand, that it suffers because of its remoteness from God. Too many citizens of the earthly city have no idea what to do to reduce their suffering. Many, panic-stricken in their distress, feverishly search a way out of the inevitable dead end of a society without God, but how many of them know the way to healing? The monastic city does not see itself as a sort of Noah's ark, but rather as a place to lie at anchor, or as a point of reference, a lighthouse that warns of reefs and shows the way to safety. The monk is also a sort of lookout who already sees the shore and, by the good news he announces and by the evidence of his joy, brings comfort and hope to the crew. The monastic city can also be compared, in a way, to a great hospital complex, with a quasi-sacred precinct and a mysterious and elaborate structure, which excite a paradoxical mixture of fear and dread along with a sense of protection and security. It is a strange but most beneficial place, where weakness is neighbor to strength, fragility to dexterity, lassitude to courage, death to life. Beyond doubt a *locus terribilis*, the monastery is at the same time a place of suffering and healing, of human misery and devotion to duty, a place of both burial and resurrection.

Visibly cut off, the monastic city is in reality an independent commonwealth, a free city, a city open to God's infinitude. As it belongs to the earth, its base is as solid as can be, but its foundation can also be imagined as an inverted pyramid whose wide base is rooted in heaven. After all, if all the various ziggurats, like the too famous tower of Babel, which the world has always tried to build, are results of the pride of man seeking to seize hold of heaven, it might be possible to consider that monasteries, scattered among hollows and valleys, are results of the humility of God, seeking among the children of men simple, faithful and unpretentious souls, who will persevere and pray in the humble service of loving presence to which God calls them.

This hiding in the ground that raises up, and this solitude that brings near, are perhaps not the least of the paradoxes of the monastic city. Having made his heart firm in God, the monk finds himself liberated from material things, from all creation, from his fellows. He does not look for idols in this passing world, but he does recognize the hand of God there. This is undoubtedly his secret. If the monk takes himself to the desert, away from the world and the mob, this is neither desertion of the earthly city nor a flight from his responsibilities. If it were, his disdain for all that is human and liable to decay would never have led him to develop the land, hew stone and recopy thousands and thousands of manuscripts, by no means all of which transmit eternal truths. The monk cares for his surroundings and despises only that which destroys God's handiwork. Lack of respect for a healthy hierarchy of values, of which the idols of every age and heart are the origin and the distressing consequence, brings in its wake disdain and forgetfulness of God, something that no Christian can accept. The monk is one of those who seek to recognize and manifest in the world the sovereignty of God, and to render to everything else only the importance that is proportionate to the end for which it was created.

The earthly city no longer has any definite idea of where it is going, where it has come from, and what it is. Where indeed is the modern city headed, that city which, like every city, never ceases to run this way and that, stirs itself up, panics, yet fails to advance an inch, and often falls back. Where is this crippled city bound, as it hides from its own unbearable pain?

Blessed is the city of the Christian, blessed is the city of the Church, blessed is the monastic city founded on the rock, in which the height and the lightness of the church building give enthusiasm to the heart, and where the sturdiness of the stone gives gravity and weight, a weight which does not weight down, which does not hamper the pace but rather gives it assurance, encourages and brings back to the essential, to the essential of eternal certitudes.

Is Romanesque art a typically monastic form of art? It is not entirely surprising that many of our contemporaries are struck by this austere art which seems perfectly suited to Gregorian chant. What can elevate the heart more than a Romanesque crypt? Man needs to descend into his interior depths, into the secret place of his heart, to live with himself in order to be reconciled with God at last and to live in communion with his brothers.

Beata vita, visio pacis!

NOTES

1. The eighteenth century saw the discovery of the stone altars, today in the Musée de Cluny, which testify to the construction of a pagan temple dedicated to Jupiter, probably during the reign of Tiberius, at the time of Christ, on the present site of the choir of the cathedral. Cf. P.M. Auzas, Notre Dame de Paris (Paris: Hachette, 1956), p. 14.

2. The motto of the city of Paris, whose emblem is a ship: "It is tossed by the waves, but does not sink." The origin of this motto lies in the comparison between the Ile de la Cité and a ship.

3. Painting on parchment, executed between 1452 and 1456. The manuscript is now in the Metropolitan Museum of New York, Ms 194. One of the best and most accessible modern reproductions is in Willibald Sauerlander, *Le monde gothique. Le siècle des cathédrales, 1140-1260*, in the series *L'univers des formes* (Paris: Gallimard, 1989), pp. 154 155.

4. Cf. pp. 31-56, especially pp. 50 and 51 of Summer McK. Crosby, *L'abbaye royale de Saint-Denis* (Paris: Hartman, 1953), a well-researched

work completing an earlier book by the same author, *The abbey of Saint-Denis 475-1122* (New Haven: Yale University Press, 1942).

5. First edition: Oxford: Basil Blackwell, 1966; second edition: Oxford: Mowbray, 1977. The French edition is part of the series *Spiritualité Orientale*, n. 31, (Abbaye de Bellefontaine, 1980).

6. Athanasius, *Vie d'Antoine*, 14.7, edited and with commentary by J.M. Bartelink, *Sources Chrétiennes*, no. 400, (Paris: Cerf, 1994), p 174. For the Latin text: Ch. Mohrmann, *Vita di Antonio* (Rome, 1974), p. 38; A. Wilmart, "Une version inédite de la Vie de S. Antoine," in *Revue Bénédictine*, no. 31, 1914, pp. 163-173; G. Garitte, *Un témoin important du texte de la Vie de S. Antoine par S. Athanase: la version latine inédite des archives du Chapitre de Saint-Pierre à Rome* (Brussels-Rome, 1939); Ch. Mohrmann, "Note sur la version latine la plus ancienne de la Vie de S. Antoine par S. Athanase," in *Studia Anselmiana*, no. 38, 1956, pp. 35-44; A. de Vogüé, *Histoire littéraire du mouvement monastique dans l'Antiquité* (Paris: Cerf, 1991), p. 89, note 33.

7. A. Guillaumont, *Aux origines du monachisme chrétien*, Series *Spiritualité Orientale*, no. 30 (Bellefontaine, 1979), p. 153.

8. Cf. Jean Cassian, *Institutions cénobitiques*, *Sources Chrétiennes*, no. 109 (Paris: Cerf, 1965), pp. 122-123, n. 1; P. Ladeuze, *Etude sur le cénobitisme pakhomien pendant le quatrième siècle et la première partie du cinquième siècle* (Paris-Louvain, 1898), pp. 202-204; cf. Chitty, *op. cit.* (French translation), p. 65.

9. Number suggested by J. Maspero, quoted in P. Cousin, *Précis d'histoire monastique* (Paris: Bloud et Gay, 1956), p. 57.

10. *Epître à Héliodore*, ed. J. Labourt, (Paris: Les Belles Lettres, 1949), p. 44. For this quotation and theme, cf. E.C. Amelineau, "Vie Copte de Macaire," in *Annales du Musée Guimet* (Paris, 1894), XXV, p. 65; *Apophthegmata Patrum*, Isaac: 5; C.J.M. Bartelink, "Les oxymores desertum civitatis et desertum floribus vernans," in *Studia Monastica*, 1973, XV, pp. 7-15.

11. Cf. Chitty, *op. cit.*, p. 67.

12. Letter 18; cf. Dom E. Martène, *Thesaurus Novus Anecdotorum*, vol. 1, 1717, p. 494; Dom R. Ceillier, *Histoire Générale des Auteurs sacrés et ecclésiastiques* (Paris, 1963), vol. 14, p. 410. In favor of the identification with the author of *Microcosmus*, cf. Ceillier, *ibid.*, vol. 15, p. 811, and against this identification, P. Delhaye, *Le Microcosmus de Godefroy de Saint-Victor*, (Lille, 1951), p. 43ff.

13. For a general view of monastic intellectual activity, the transmission of culture and monks' civilizing role, the most useful works are: Dom U. Berlière, *L'ordre monastique des origines au douzième siècle*, series *Pax*, no. 1 (Paris-Lille, 1924); Dom J. Leclercq, *L'amour des lettres et le*

désir de Dieu, (Paris, 1957); P. Riche, "Education et culture dans l'Occident barbare," *Patristica Sorbonensia,* no. 4 (Paris, 1962); P. Riche, *Ecoles et enseignement dans le Haut Moyen Age* (Paris, 1979); Various authors, *Benedictini vivendi praeceptores, Actes du Colloque de Pédagogie bénédictine* (Maredsous, 1981); A.G. Hamman, *L'epopée du livre. Du scribe à l'imprimerie* (Paris, 1985).

14. An excellent short book that highlights the impact and equilibrium of the Rule of St. Benedict, and its application to those who are neither monks nor nuns is: E. de Waal, *Seeking God: The Way of St. Benedict* (London: Fount, 1984).

15. Rule of St. Benedict, 58.15-16.

16. Rule of St. Benedict, 66.6-7.

17. Dom P. Delatte, *Commentaire sur la Règle de Saint Benoît* (Paris, 1913), pp. 532-533.

18. On monastic art in general and on the contrast between Cluniac and Cistercian art in particular, see the well-researched and balanced contribution of Henry-Bernard de Warren, "Bernard et les premiers cisterciens face au problème de l'art," in *Bernard de Clairvaux,* edited by the Central Historical Commission of the Order of Cîteaux (Paris: Alsatia, 1953), pp. 487-534.

19. Tob. 13:21 (Latin); Common of the Dedication of a Church, antiphon at Lauds and Vespers.

20. Gradual of the Epiphany.

21. *Apophthegms,* Alphabetical Series, Arsenius 13.

22. A. Guillaumont, "La conception du desert chez les moines d'Egypte," in *Revue de l'histoire des religions,* vol. 188 (Paris, 1975), reprinted in *Aux origines...* (cf. n. 7).

23. On this subject, see R.-G. Coquin, "Evolution du monachisme égyptien," in *Le monde copte,* nos. 21-22, 1993, p. 15, and Guillaumont, "Esquisse d'une phénoménologie du monachisme," in *Numen,* vol. 25 (Leiden, 1978), reprinted in *Aux origines...* (cf. n. 7).

24. Rule of St. Benedict, 4.75.

25. Dorotheus of Gaza, *Oeuvres spirituelles,* translated Dom L. Regnault and Dom J. de Préville, *Sources Chrétiennes,* no. 92 (Paris: Cerf, 1963), Instruction 6.77, p. 285.

26. Cf. Gn. 28:17; Common of the Dedication of a Church, Second Vespers, Magnificat antiphon.

"BUILDING ITSELF THROUGH LOVE": THE MONASTERY AS ESCHATOLOGICAL CITY

Bernard Bonowitz, OCSO

*(St. Joseph's Abbey,
Spencer, Massachusetts)*

Benedictine monks are migrants. A great dynamism pushes them forward to the possession of God's kingdom. From the Prologue of the Rule where we meet them, they are up (8) and running (13), and at the conclusion where we take leave of them they are still "hastening to their heavenly homeland" (73.8).

Yet the image that immediately suggests itself—a long, winding vista with individual monks at different places along the way between the starting gate and the finish line—is not the most appropriate one to describe their journey. Rather, the truest picture of their pilgrimage is one taken from the Psalms of Ascent: a city made compact in unity (Ps. 121:3). A Benedictine monastery journeys from earth to heaven by becoming a *koinonia*.

The name coenobium, "life in common," bestowed on it in Chapter One of the Rule, is also its way to God and ultimately its goal. Progress towards the kingdom thus consists of increasing consolidation of mind and heart and, to the extent that this unity in faith and love is achieved, the community already enters the kingdom and itself becomes the eschatological city. This is why Benedict's description of the monastic koinonia in Chapter 72 glides so gently into its conclusion: "And may He bring us all together into everlasting life" (72.12). The city of peace opens into the city of heavenly vision.

How is this koinonia formed? It is important to see that the various exigencies imposed by the Rule have as their aim the construction of a *congregatio* in which the whole life of all the members is joined together to become a dwelling place for God in the Spirit. From the time of a monk's entrance into the community, the Rule lays claim to his personhood level by level, detaching him from himself and pouring him into the common life, so that finally he can be found only in *congregatione*. Before the monk both comprehends and consents to this "transfusion," his reaction to the Rule's slow but unremitting work of incorporating him into the monastic fellowship is marked by fear and reluctance. But once he catches on, rather than simply submitting to the process of "koinonization," he actively fosters it. Having grasped that his life is not being poured into the sand but used for building the very city he is seeking, he becomes zealous, and with a good zeal. It is here that the passage from the constricted heart to the expanded heart referred to in the Prologue (48-9) takes place.

Let us consider more specifically the particular ways in which the monastic *conversatio* established by the Rule takes hold of an incoming monk to draw him into the charity of the fraternity (72.8). Perhaps in doing this the most appropriate method is to proceed from the more external to the more internal claims. Although the communal life impinges on new members in various ways right from the beginning, I think it is legitimate to speak of a "history of sensation." Only with time does the monk become aware that the community is the circle of friends for whom he is supposed to lay down his life—with no strings attached. Granted this can be said to him in his first days of the novitiate and that he too may employ such ultimate language very early on to describe what the community requires of him; nevertheless, because he enters the community with the unconscious conviction that so much of his life is permanently, non-negotiably his, he will initially experience the summons to self-donation only to the degree that this is imaginable for him. To clarify my point from my work as vocation director in our community: Many candidates, no matter what you tell them about the *dura et aspera*, can grasp this only in terms of what they can bring, how often they can write and who can come to see them on their family visits. So, beginning from the outer layers:

1. *Possessions*: In line with the foregoing monastic tradition (recall the opening chapters of Book IV of the *Institutes* and Chapter One of the Rule of St. Augustine), St. Benedict is deter-

mined that "property"—objects that are one's own, one's *pro-prium*—not exist in the monastery, but that everything belong to the community: *Omnia sint communia* (33.6). (A small but interesting indication of the Rule's vehemence on this point can be found in the relevant chapter titles. Among the many *De*'s and *Qualis*'s that introduce the chapter headings, there are only four beginning with *Si*—whether—and three of these have to do with private ownership [33, 34, 54]. It is as if Benedict were hoping to be explicitly asked if a monk might own something so that he could give a resounding "No.")

What are the reasons for this insistence? First of all, in abolishing private property, Benedict turns a collection of self-reliant owners into a family circle, all looking with confident hope to the father of the community to supply their needs (*omnia vera necessaria a patre sperare monasterii*, 33.5; cf. Ps. 103:27 [Vg.]. *Omnia in te sperant ut des cibum eis in tempore suo*). Furthermore, as the brothers observe the abbot apportioning the monastery's goods, they are initiated into a social principle of distribution—not favoritism, but consideration of needs. The recognition that in the monastery each person's genuine requirements are not only being noticed but justly met creates a pervading sense of peace and unity. Benedict expresses this in the words, "Thus all the members will be in peace" (34.5), the sole, and very apposite, use of the Pauline image of *membra* in the Rule.

2. *Bodies*: Benedict associates the surrender of private ownership to the community with the monks giving up "the free disposal (*in propria voluntate*) of their bodies and wills" (33.4). The monk learns that his body is always expected somewhere, and that this somewhere is determined by a foundational concern of the Rule, namely, that the monks constantly enact, and thereby stabilize and strengthen, the koinonia. In a Benedictine monastery, the community as a whole attends the Office, takes its meals together—and does the kitchen chores together afterwards—gathers for the reading before Compline, etc. For all the places where Benedict is willing to make allowances so that the weak have nothing to flee from, he is quite strict when it comes to tardiness at the Office and at table (the fact that the Rule has a

long chapter dedicated to this question demonstrates its importance). In his view, lateness makes it impossible, not only for the tardy individual, but for everyone in the community, "to pray and come to table" as they should—*sub uno* (43.13). The common table of which the Rule speaks is actually the gathering of the brothers to give thanks and eat together, and when monks are absent "through their own negligence and fault" (43.14), although the others do pray and eat, for that meal at least there is no *mensa communis*.

There are other ways in which the monk discovers that his body is not his own. Needs of the community workforce may result in his being shuffled from one employment to another (53.18-20); the community's fiscal situation may require him to work longer and harder than the horarium has led him to expect (48.7). All of these expropriations will inevitably provoke a crisis of attitude. How is the monk to interiorly live this state of affairs where he must constantly be at the disposal of *their* schedule, *their* endeavors, the holes and needs created through other monks' illnesses and absences or by an unusual number of outside guests?

3. *Will*: Perhaps this is why Benedict links in a single phrase the renunciation of control over one's body and control over one's will. The irritation produced by the community's assimilating action, the frustration that must surface at not being able to "do what I want when I want as I want" forces a decision: either the will follows the body into the koinonia or it signals the body and together they return to the world. A "middle" possibility—indefinitely extending the unresolved situation of a body that does what it's told while the heart keeps its own resentful counsel—Benedict will not tolerate. That "solution" he calls murmuring, and his references to it (5.17,18 and *passim*) make clear that he considers it as evil a vice as private property. In encouraging an open-hearted obedience, moreover, the Rule does not argue on the basis of the good of an abstract self-transcendence. Instead, in some beautiful phrases, it demonstrates the blessing a willing obedience bestows on those to whom it is extended (*dulcis hominibus*, 5.14), and how its reciprocal exercise is one of

the most dynamic elements in the intensification of true communal life (*Oboedientia sibi certatim impendant, nullus quod sibi utile iudicat sequatur, sed quod magis alio,* 72.6-7). In other words, the love that makes monks "eager to take the narrow road" of obedience (5.10) is love of the brotherhood at the same time that it is love of God.

4. *Affectivity:* Nor does the Rule draw a line here. Having claimed the individual's goods, body and will for the communal life, it reaches more deeply into the person, as it must if the community of believers is to grow into one mind and one heart. The monk is asked at the conclusion of Chapter Four (4.64-73) to commit himself to a transformation of his desire and aggression that will foster an environment of fraternal affection. The kind of selfless love which Benedict encourages and which he refers to as "chastity" has as its hallmark the spontaneous capacity to give each person in the community what he can most gladly and easily receive: his due. For the elder monks there is reverence, expressing itself through such little marks of respect as special forms of greeting and giving up one's seat (63.12,15-16), for the younger, an affectionate solicitude, for the abbot a regard that is both deferential and unconstrained. To arrive at this habit of discerning charity, Benedict realizes, requires a resolution to root out the various internal and external forms of hostility: hatred, jealousy, arrogance, quarreling (4.65-69). This in turn presumes an extended discipline of all anger-driven behavior, whether this manifests itself through verbal violence, avoidance or superficiality (4.22-28). The monk has to learn to become a stranger to all these ways of acting that come from the *saeculum*, "this present age" (4.20) and find a way of interacting that incarnates an absolute preference for Christ (4.21). Within the context of the common life, that preference will translate itself into the pursuit of peace, a pursuit so swift and determined that it reaches and reconciles the opponent before the sun goes down (4.73).

5. *Thoughts:* While the community experiences firsthand the enrichment and elevation of its life that comes about through the conversion of manners just described, there are certain aspects of

the monk's self-entrustment of which they can have only an indirect knowledge. According to the fifth step of humility, the monk manifests to his abbot all his sinful thoughts as well as any wrongs he has committed in secret (7.44). How does this represent a move from isolation into the communal life? To begin with, as in the case of distribution of goods, it connects him very closely to the father of the monastery. Just as there his physical poverty expressed a confident dependence, shared with every other brother, that the abbot as head of the community would provide for all his needs (and everyone else's), so the revelation of secret thoughts as portrayed by St. Benedict is a presentation of the monk's interior poverty that confidently looks for forgiveness and healing (7.45-48). Surely it is no accident that the two occasions that the monk is described as hoping for something (*sperare*) from the abbot occur in reference to the expropriation of goods and the manifestation of secret thoughts (33.5; 7.45). Secondly, no matter how privately this process—the "middle range" of the ladder of humility—begins, it moves to a very common and visible conclusion. For the sixth step finds the brother contented with whatever treatment is meted out to him, the seventh brings him to the heartfelt conviction that he is of less value than all the rest, and the eighth confirms him in the monastery's common rule and his superiors' example (7.55). By handing over his secrets to the abbot, he has also handed in his separateness, his living "apart from." Therefore, in return, he not only receives the personal advice and consolation of the abbot, he becomes penetrated by the monastery's ways and discovers that his ways are the ways of the community. Or more accurately, the rest of the community discovers it. "He is becoming a monk," they say.

6. *Judgment*: There is a chapter in the Rule that quietly depicts both the depth and the totality of the monk's vocation to be at the community's disposal: Chapter 68, "Assignment of Impossible Tasks." The situation is one where the brother, who has first accepted "with complete gentleness and obedience" a mandate given him by the abbot, finds in attempting to fulfill it that "the weight of the burden is altogether too much for his strength"

(68.1-2). Benedict allows and in fact encourages him to take the opportune moment to explain the circumstances to the abbot. Yet if the abbot holds to what he has ordered, *sciat iunior ita sibi expediat, et ex caritate, confidens de adiutorio Dei, oboediat* (68.4-5). Not only is the monk to take up once more the burden that his own back had taught him was overwhelming, he is to believe in the superior's judgment ("Let him recognize that this is best for him") over the private conclusions of his experience. In this moment, payment on the choice the brother made when he entered the monastery to live by another's judgment (*alieno iudicio*, 5.12) falls due. Even beyond this, the junior "must in *love* obey"—in love for the abbot and the community that will be served by this particular sacrifice. It is such situations that draw out of the brother a monastic form of fidelity to the Great Commandment (*ex toto corde, tota anima, tota virtute*) which Benedict puts at the head of the instruments of good works (4.1).

Having accompanied the monk in his various stages of migration into the koinonia—deprivatization of goods, body, will, emotions, thoughts, judgment—the reader may wonder if active cooperation in this incorporation is really mandatory for the members of a monastic community. The answer I think is contained in one of the names Benedict gives to his monastery: *domus Dei*, the house of God (31.19). What does this title imply? That while the monastery is not yet fully the city of God, it *is* His home. To enter it is to leave the world behind, to step into an environment where, like it or not, the terrestrial, the secular, simply does not exist as a possible *modus vivendi*. Because it is the *domus Dei* the monastery operates on heavenly principles; a tremendous divine energy quietly exercises its authority on everyone and everything with the single intention of forming all in the house into a community ripe for heaven. This is the community we see exposed to our gaze in Chapter 72, a vision which for the cenobite is almost as evocative and satisfying as the picture of the New Jerusalem in the Apocalypse. In other words, the monastery is, somehow, celestial, and to the celestial the only alternative is the infernal.

One of the guiding insights of the Rule of St. Benedict is that when it comes to personal and spiritual realities, "the way up is down" (*Per humilitatem ascenditur; humilitate ascendere;* 7.5,7). The purpose of this article has been to suggest that the way up is "in" as well, to the center of the community. We know from reading and scholarship that Cassian and others claimed an apostolic origin for the cenobitic life. It is for our experience to trace its origins further and see for ourselves what Baldwin of Ford discovered, that the roots and power of the common life come from the angelic *consortium* and the trinitarian communion. Compact in unity, the monastic city is drawn up into its source.

A MONASTIC CITY WITHIN THE SECULAR CITY: THE ENGLISH CATHEDRAL PRIORY

Aidan Bellenger
*(Downside Abbey,
Bath, England)*

Many European cathedrals stand magnificently on hilltops and in the center of cities but few outside England capture the special character of the English Cathedral close. A close is a distinct precinct area, fortified without and domestic within, forming in many cases a city within a city. Many of these closes were enhanced by the domesticity forced by the clerical marriages and families of the Reformation, but in essence they were the creation of the Middle Ages. Such notable cathedral closes as Salisbury and Wells were the setting for the comings and goings of the many dignitaries and officials who proliferated in the shadow of great secular foundations under their deans and chapters. They were to provide the inspiration for Anthony Trollope's "Barchester" novels. Others, however, began life as monastic enclosures, a monastic city within the secular city, a cathedral monastery, a peculiarly English institution which, despite the inevitable clash of jurisdictions, had a resilience as an ideal which lasted until the present century.

The arrival of St Augustine and his missionary monks in Kent in 597 and the subsequent spread of Christianity in the south of England from Canterbury made an early identification between monk and bishop a characteristic feature of the *Ecclesia Anglicana*, but it was not until the tenth century with the great reform movement in the English Church led by monks that the concept of the cathedral monastery received its definitive shape. The great reforming prelates of the tenth century revival were monk-bishops like Ethelwold of Winchester who sought to reform their cathedral clergy by making them into monks and to make their cathedral churches not only the liturgical centers of their dioceses but houses of observant and continuous praise. By the time of the Norman Conquest after 1066, the cathedrals of Canterbury, Sherborne (later an abbey following the translation of its *Cathedra* to Ramsbury and Sarum), Winchester, and Worcester, had chapters consisting of Benedictine monks under the normal government of a prior with the bishop as abbot.

The Normans had a genius for making the best Anglo-Saxon institutions their own and many of the most gifted new bishops, like their Anglo-Saxon predecessors, were monks. These included Lanfranc of Canterbury and William of St Carlilef of Durham. They had shared in the great expansion of monastic life in Normandy where monasticism was seen as the most dynamic instrument of reform. The Norman abbey of Bec, of which Lanfranc and his great successor Anselm were monks, became the nursery of many of the first generation of Anglo-Norman bishops. Such men were instrumental in expanding the idea and practice of the cathedral priory and by 1133 when Carlisle (which with its Augustinian canons was the only such foundation not to be Benedictine) became a monastic cathedral, there were monastic chapters at Bath, Coventry, Durham, Ely, Norwich and Rochester as well as at the Anglo-Saxon foundations. Bath and Coventry were endowed as second cathedrals in the dioceses of Wells and Lichfield which both had an existing cathedral with a secular charter.

Canterbury, the focal point of the English church, had, throughout the Middle Ages, a cathedral priory which was in the first rank of English monastic houses. Its buildings were on a formidable scale. Its church, the cathedral, with a splendid late twelfth-century choir, was adjoined by a cloister rebuilt by Prior Chillenden (1390-1411) with 825 heraldic bosses on its vault commemorating its benefactors. The chapter house was both lofty and spacious while the dormitory for the monks, built by Lanfranc, and measuring 148 ft. by 78 ft. continued to serve its original purpose until the dissolution of the monastery by Henry VIII in 1540. Such surroundings emphasized the pre-eminence of a community whose monastic roots went back to the sixth century. St Augustine seems to have lived a quasi-monastic life with his fellow monks from Rome and the secular clerks who assisted him in his household. The foundation by St Augustine of an abbey just outside the city walls, dedicated to St Peter and St Paul, intended as a burial place for his successors and for the Kings of Kent, reduced the strictly monastic element in the episcopal church and in the seventh century, under Abbot Adrian, St Peter and St Paul (its dedication was extended by St Dunstan in 978 to include St Augustine, by which name it is now known) became one of the great centers of religion and learning in England. In the early years of the seventh century, Archbishop Laurence established a full monastic life in the Christ Church community, but with the accession of Theodore of Tarsus in 668, Christ Church Cathedral was provided with a secular chapter. It was to remain like this until 997 when Archbishop Aelfric (995-1005), returning from Rome with his pallium, replaced the canons with monks, it is said, at papal command.

When Lanfranc consolidated the monastery he had solid traditions and foundations to build on. Lanfranc hoped for 150 monks in his community, a number attained briefly by about 1125. At most times the numbers were nearer to seventy or eighty with a low point of less than thirty at the end of the thirteenth century. Archbishop Lanfranc's Constitutions for the cathedral monastery, conflated from "the customaries of several of the most celebrated and fervent houses" of the day, as Dom David Knowles puts it in his introduction to his translation of the Constitutions, provides us with a unique insight into the ideals of the monastic life of the period. Christ Church, Canterbury, was to be in the vanguard of reform. Under Lanfranc the cathedral priory ideal was at its greatest flowering, not least because the archbishops were abbots *de facto* as well as *de iure*, living the common life with their brethren. This was the intention of both Ethelwold and Lanfranc, the two principal architects of the idea.

At Canterbury, as elsewhere, the system worked well, as long as the archbishop was a monk or sympathetic to monks. Thus under Lanfranc and Anselm, and to a lesser extent under Theobald and Thomas Becket (who although not a monk liked to live as one during the rare moments of peace he was allowed) Canterbury Cathedral monastery enjoyed prosperity. In the centuries that followed, the clashes between the monks and the archbishops, and between the Crown and the archbishop and the monks, became more furious. In a whole complex of jurisdictions their major area of conflict was over the appointment of archbishops. Within the monastic, Benedictine tradition, it is the monks who elect their abbot, who in turn appoints the prior and the senior obedientiaries and monastic officials. At Christ Church, Canterbury, their abbot was also Archbishop of Canterbury, Metropolitan and Primate of All England. Although in the end some compromises were reached whereby the monks elected their cathedral prior whose role became increasingly abbatial (symbolized by his right to *pontificalia*) *en route* there were many bitter disagreements. Perhaps the most fierce was the disputed election following the death of Archbishop Hubert Walter in 1205 during the reign of King John which led, directly, to the imposition of Papal Interdict on England from 1208-1213 and to the temporary dispersal of the monastery. This state of affairs was triggered by the desire of the monks to elect one of their own to the throne of St Augustine.

I have concentrated on Canterbury because of its pre-eminent position, but similar examples of disputes could be cited for all the other houses. At Durham, for example, the great northern exemplar of Cathedral monasticism, which came under Benedictine administration in 1083, Bishop Hugh de Puiset (elected in 1153), was involved in forty years of conflict with the cathedral monks over his claim to appoint their prior and his right to the custody of the priory's parish churches. It would be too simplistic to conclude that the whole life of these cathedral priories was one of strife, but it is obvious that the constitutional difficulties inherent in a closed monastic community in tandem with a bishop drawn from the secular clergy and with outside political interests was a recipe for difficulties if not disaster.

Under Henry VIII, the cathedral priories were closed although they survived institutionally by transformation into secular foundations. In some cases, as at Winchester, the last Cathedral Prior became the first Dean. Monastic life did not remain dormant for long and one of the monks of Mary Tudor's briefly revived Westminster Abbey, Sigebert Buckley, is said to have "aggregated" two of the members of the old English Benedictine Congregation to the new one which was stirring into life in the first quarter of the seventeenth century. The bull *Plantata*, issued by Pope Urban VIII in 1633, gave to the revived congregation all the rights and privileges of the old congregation including the right to the former cathedral priories. The bull carried little real weight, but as far as cathedral priories were concerned it gave support to the English Benedictines against the claim of Bishop Richard Smith, Vicar Apostolic of England, to have Ordinary jurisdiction over the regulars in England. The English Benedictine General Chapter in 1629 had appointed nine cathedral priors ready to re-occupy their stalls when England should return to the Catholic fold and also claimed the three cathedrals erected by Henry VIII from the dissolved monasteries of Chester, Gloucester and Peterborough.

In 1629 the capitular fathers saw the priors as true officials exercising jurisdiction and throughout the seventeenth and eighteenth centuries they held a stranglehold on the proceedings of the General Chapter of the Congregation. Cathedral Priors are still (1994) appointed by the President of the English Benedictine Congregation (the E.B.C.) but as titles of honor given to distinguished members of the congregation. Even so, according to the existing constitutions of the EBC, the Cathedral Priors of Canterbury, Winchester and Durham are given precedence. In English Benedictine circles the Middle Ages died hard. It is not surprising that in the nineteenth century with a number of English Benedictine communities domiciled in England after centuries of exile that the idea of reviving the model of the cathedral monastery re-emerged. In the more recent history of the English Benedictines there have been two attempts at establishing a cathedral priory: at Belmont in Herefordshire and at Westminster. The first was successful for a time, the second abortive.

Belmont, which lies on the side of the city of Hereford towards Wales, itself a cathedral city with a secular foundation, was in a rural setting in the Victorian period although in recent years urban sprawl and especially "out-of-town" supermarkets have brought it just within the city boundaries. Its church, with its prominent central tower, began life as the suitably Gothic revival thank-offering of a wealthy convert, Francis Richard Wegg-Prosser, and it was only gradually that the plan emerged of making it the monastic cathedral of the diocese of Newport and Menevia, the Catholic diocese then for Wales, whose bishop, Thomas Joseph Brown, was a monk (of Downside). Brown saw the whole of Wales as a suitable place for a Benedictine mission and Wegg-Prosser's church as an ideal physical setting for his *cathedra*. In 1851 Brown was hoping to persuade his own monastic *conventus* to transfer from Somerset to Hereford. By April 1852 a Benedictine monastic chapter for Newport and Menevia was established. In 1853 Belmont was offered as a Cathedral and in the following year the EBC General Chapter agreed to Belmont as a common house of studies. In 1859 a cathedral priory with full rights was appointed and in 1860 the church was consecrated with great solemnity.

The emphasis on Belmont as a Cathedral for the full monastic liturgy was made apparent by the invitation of the Abbot of Solesmes, the prophet of liturgical rectitude, to pontificate at the Mass of Dedication on 4 September 1860. He had arrived the day before. "It is said," writes Dom Basil Whelan, "that as he knew that traveling in the Benedictine habit would not be tolerated in England, he dressed in what he conceived would be suitable clerical garb, and on arriving at Gloucester station on the evening of September 3 he missed the conveyance that had been sent for him, and looked such a strange figure in baggy breeches, tight coat, and beaver hat, and unable to speak English, that he was narrowly and suspiciously questioned by the police before being sent on to Hereford." He arrived in time, however, and, according to Dom Basil, "was fully alert, for he at once asked what offices were to be sung, and being told that the First Vespers of the Dedication would be sung at once, he remarked that that was impossible as the church was not yet dedicated. In consequence the liturgy had to be changed to the office of the day, that of St Stephen of Hungary."

A high level of liturgical correctness and a full conventual life were to be characteristic of the Cathedral Priory of Belmont which was officially a Pro-Cathedral from 1855 and a full Cathedral from 1916. The difficulties which the arrangements encountered were similar to those encountered by the priory's medieval antecedents. When, in 1916, the Archdiocese of Cardiff was erected, Belmont had to share the bishop's throne with Cardiff. In 1920 the monastic chapter was abolished and Belmont became an autonomous abbey within the English Benedictine Congregation.

Belmont's comparative physical isolation distinguished it from the medieval cathedral monasteries and was seen as a weakness from the beginning. "If it is at some out of the way place," the formidable Benedictine bishop of Birmingham, Ullathorne reflected on the situation of the Welsh Cathedral, "it will be a sham.... Take hold of Newport, and you take hold of the diocese." Moreover the years of the Belmont Cathedral monastery coincided with the transformation of the English Benedictine Congregation from a centralized religious order into a network of autonomous abbeys. Belmont, with its common house of studies and its inherent lack of independence owing to its reliance on the local bishop, did not fit into the new scheme of things. It is ironical, however, that it was at Belmont in its then unparalleled magnificence of setting that a full, conventual life was experienced by the English Benedictines for the first time since the Dissolution.

Westminster Abbey, briefly a Cathedral under Henry VIII and afterwards a collegiate church with Dean and Chapter, was the monastery which above all symbolized the monastic presence at the heart of the nation, a city within a city. It is not surprising that when Cardinal Herbert Vaughan, who had two Benedictine brothers and was himself partly educated at Downside, was looking into the management of his new cathedral at Westminster, that his thoughts turned to a Benedictine presence in the cathedral. The foundation stone of the new church, the most ambitious structure to be designed for Catholic worship since the Reformation, was blessed in the summer of 1895 and in the following year the Cardinal invited the Downside Benedictines to open a house at Ealing in the western suburbs of London at least in part to "be sufficiently near to Westminster to contribute to the choral services of the Cathedral." The Ealing community was to develop eventually into an abbey. The Westminster scheme encountered difficulties, again reflecting medieval precedents, in the relations between the secular clergy, especially the existing Westminster chapter, and in the nature of monastic independence. Vaughan's negotiations with Abbot Paul Delatte of Solesmes to provide a monastic choir for the cathedral also failed. In the end in 1902 Downside's lay music master, Richard (later Sir Richard) Terry, was appointed Master of the Cathedral

Music and established the musical context of a rich and full celebration of the liturgy.

The secular city and the monastic city do not make easy partners and it is not surprising that the idea of the cathedral monastery with all its jurisdictional complications, was not entirely satisfactory. Yet, at its heart, the idea was a good one, siting a house of prayer at the heart of the bishop's church. It is not surprising that many contemporary bishops see the central importance of a monastic community as the powerhouse of prayer for their diocese and that many of them have established monastic houses in the heart of the city.

NOTE

R.A.L. Smith has looked at *Canterbury Cathedral Priory* (Cambridge, 1943) and R.B. Dobson at *Durham Priory 1400-1450* (Cambridge 1973). Both emphasize the administrative life of the communities as does B. Harvey in *Westminster Abbey and its Estates in the Middle Ages* (Oxford, 1977). The same author's more recent work, *Living and Dying in England, 1100-1540. The Monastic Experience* (Oxford, 1993) looks at Westminster again and provides an insight into the daily life of the members of a medieval urban Benedictine Community. D. Knowles, *The Monastic Order in England* (Cambridge, 1940), pp. 129-134, and C.H. Lawrence, *Medieval Monasticism* (London, 1984), pp. 120-123 give good general surveys of the Medieval Cathedral monasteries. I have used D. Lunn, *The English Benedictines 1540-1688* (London, 1980), especially Chapter 4, for the revival of the concept of cathedral priories in the seventeenth century, B. Whelan, *The History of Belmont Abbey (England)* (London, 1959), for the Belmont Cathedral Priory, and R. Kollar, *Westminster Cathedral: From Dream to Reality* (Edinburgh, 1987) for the Westminster Scheme. D. Knowles' edition of *The Monastic Constitutions of Lanfranc* was published in 1951. A good short history and description of existing buildings of the cathedral priories is available in L. Butler and C. Given-Wilson, *Medieval Monasteries of Great Britain* (London, 1979).

URBAN MONASTICISM TODAY: WHY?*

Jean Leclercq, OSB
(Abbaye St.-Maurice,
Clervaux, Luxembourg)

Actuality of Monasticism

There is no need for a long explanation of what monasticism is. We need only to state precisely the sense in which this term will be used here, then to show to what extent it belongs to our times.

All words, in the course of history, become worn out or, what sometimes comes to the same thing, take on so many different meanings that they come no longer to have any of these meanings. But whatever the historical changes of vocabulary, the juridical ambiguities of its contents, the generally accepted meaning in the Church today admits no equivocation. In the typology of the different forms of Christian existence, "monastic" is that which is centered on attentiveness to God, consequently, that which grants prayer priority over all other activities (without excluding them), and admits them in the measure that they are compatible with this fundamental attitude, this primordial occupation. Everything else (structures and observances) is only intended to facilitate this life of prayer for those who have responded to the call, as well as for those who come to seek in their communities the witness they bear to the absolute love received from God, rendered to God, through Jesus Christ, in the Holy Spirit: joyful renouncement and universal solidarity.

The constitutive function of monasticism is the service of prayer as participation in the contemplative diaconate of Christ, in his very experience of God, in the work of salvation which in virtue of this diaconate he accomplished during his life, in his sacrifice, and which he continues in his glory by sending his

Spirit, from the Father, upon the Church. If monasticism contains something of a mystery, which cannot be reduced to any justification of a certain efficacy, it is because it belongs to this mystery of prayer.

To speak of this activity and this way of life today we readily use the terms "contemplation" and "contemplative life." For example, an issue (1977) of a national journal for ministries on university campuses in the United States is entirely devoted to silence, meditation, and prayer, which the titles of four articles refer to as "contemplation" and the "contemplative attitude."[1] And one of the public lectures on current religious topics given each winter at Notre Dame of Paris was entitled by the organizers, *The Contemplative Call Today*. In many places, there appear what we now call "spontaneous monks" who, individually or in groups, not belonging to any particular institute, manifest that the contemplative trend constitutes one of the needs of today's world. Monasticism can fulfill this spiritual need that has existed in all ages, but makes itself felt more urgently today.

Urban Monasticism in Former Times

How will the monastic mystery, which is always and everywhere identical, be affected by being lived in an urban setting today? We must take a look at history in order to answer this. Here, as in every other area, tradition helps us to understand the requirements of today and of tomorrow, according to these words attributed to Confucius: "Tell me the past, and I will foretell you the future." In the first place, this retrospection will liberate us, if necessary, from any prejudice against the contemplative life led in the city. As a matter of fact, no one has ever identified the Christian desert (that religious situation in God's presence in which we participate in Christ's saving solitude) with the wilderness. We must remember that in the Apocalypse the Church is represented as a city, which must not be mistaken for the secular city, but which could include it so that it might be consecrated. The city is neither more nor less holy than the country; both are inhabited by sinners whom God wants to save. Furthermore, is not this work of salvation rather facilitated by the concentration of the means that we possess of communicating divine benefits to one another? An American specialist in religious sociology spoke recently of "the sacred nature of New York."

For many monks and nuns it has always been a matter of combining the desert experience with the proximity of the crowds. There are many dwelling places in God's contemplative house. Preference shown for city dwelling is one of the constants of its history from the very beginning.[2] Let us not forget that the creator of the ideology of the desert inhabited only by solitaries—I mean Cassian—spent the better part of his life in the large cities of the East before retiring to Marseilles in order to write, not without exaggeration, the interviews which he had obtained from the heads of the suburban communities, whom he presents as hermits of the Sahel. After him, urban monasticism experienced several successive waves of prosperity. Statistics of the vast region from the episcopal see of Tours to that of Maestricht and Tongres, which became that of Liège in 717 or 718, show that in Merovingian times most monasteries were situated "within the walls." Beginning with King Dagobert (623-639) the evolution is just the opposite.[3] But it begins again, and by the tenth century there were in Rome ten times more monasteries than there are now in the twentieth. And even before the legendary migration of the monks of Monte Casino to Rome, during the Byzantine-Gothic war of the sixth century, Rome had a hand in the diffusion of the Rule of Saint Benedict, this document which explicitly refers to its liturgy as being that of the "Roman Church," this text which creates, wherever it is adopted, a bond with the center of Christianity.

The names of railway stations, such as Liège-Guillemins or Limoges-Bénédictins, still evoke the fact that throughout the Middle Ages monasteries were situated along thoroughfares leading to densely populated centers. (Once I stayed in a suburb of Dublin which has the revealing name of "Monkstown," because an abbey was the origin of that extension of the capital of Ireland.) From the time in the thirteenth century when the universities came into existence, many communities wanted to have, in the cities where they were situated, a house which would be not only a residence for the university students, but a center of radiation, even of recruitment. This was when the Carthusians founded their house in Liège.

A new wave of urban monasticism unfurled in the seventeenth century when the Paix-Notre-Dame was founded at Liège, when Port-Royal-des-Champs founded Port-Royal of Paris. Those who dwelt in these foundations were considered solitaries. for it was understood that in order to merit this title one must, by Christian standards, be in solidarity with the whole environment as well as with the whole world.

It was not until the nineteenth century with its bucolic romanticism that we could affirm (I am not making this up): "the contemplative life can only be led in the country." And even then, as in the rural monasteries of all times, monks and nuns were the agents of what is called "the urbanization of the countryside." They brought the urban mentality with its demands for hygiene, for culture, for non-rural occupations (such as studies), without forgetting the urbanity of their manners, exactly as city-dwellers today expect to find in their secondary residence in the Forest of Ardennes or elsewhere the same conveniences as in their city apartments.

Feminine monasticism, in particular, has always been predominantly urban, and this is still the case today. Unlike priests, nuns are given to the ministry of prayer rather than to pastoral activity. Formerly in the cities, which generally were not vast, or in their neighborhood, they were well-known, such as the Recluses who lived at the expense of the city for which they made intercession. Today these centers of prayer are often ignored, and we have to admit that we have had our part in obscuring them with grilles and veils, which are no longer in use except in certain Mussulman societies. Recently in Rio de Janeiro I celebrated the Eucharist before one of these grilles, protected with long spear-like points, for which there was a twofold reason: first, dating from the eighteenth century, it is a preserved historical monument and, secondly, it was a custom introduced at the same time as other customs from the Iberian peninsula where the influence of Islam was so strong. The time has now come to put an end to all this folklore and to invent an urban monasticism for our times.

Urban Monasticism Today

Its Demands and the Conditions of its Existence

It is not more utopian today than it was in the past. It exists, it corresponds to a growing need, but it also involves new demands. It is present more and more in these populous districts where the majority of our contemporaries dwell, although an ever-increasing number of the privileged escape for the holidays or weekends to the countryside, nearby or far away, where monasteries also have a role to play. In both these environments they should remain primarily houses of prayer where vocations to prayer might develop, where the service of prayer in the Church (and not only liturgical prayer) is fulfilled along with, secondarily, other activities compatible with prayer and stemming from it: sharing the seclusion and recollection, the spiritual experience, the joy, the support needed to exercise contemporary forms of asceticism, witnessing to the possible compatibility between this life of prayer and culture.

But we have to admit that it is more difficult to be faithful to monastic life in the city than in the country, because the occasions of non-monastic activities are more numerous. An authentic urban monasticism is not possible except on certain conditions. It requires, first of all, a common conviction concerning the vocation and the identity, the meaning and the role of such a monasticism: a conviction concerning the life of prayer, the significance of the urban phenomenon, the monastic physiognomy that it should present. This common program will be what keeps monks and nuns functional and will make their monastery a center of attraction and not of dispersion. Certain individuals must have the courage not to undertake, at least normally, activities that are incompatible with this community vocation. It goes without saying that this conviction must be shared not only on the idealistic level but on the plane of effective charity. It does not exclude different personal convictions in many areas, they should even be an asset to it; but there is no monastic testimony where union of hearts is not perceptible.

This basic conviction should necessarily be accompanied by an observance adapted to the urban environment and not conceived for a rural milieu, as formerly. This entails practical consequences, first of all as concerns the timetable where it is especially evident. It is no longer affected, as was the case up until the nineteenth century, by the natural length of days and nights, but by what has been called "industrial time," that is, the result of human industry. Everywhere gas or electricity has, according to the psalm, "changed night into day." As for the rhythms of life, they no longer result solely from the succession of the seasons, nor of the week and of Sunday, but from the alternation of periods, shorter but more intense than formerly, of productive work and of vacations, with their possibility of contemplative leisure. The seventh-day rest has been replaced by the long weekend which begins the evening of the fifth day. Monasteries in the city will receive more guests and exercise hospitality in a different manner from Monday until Thursday, while those in the country will be frequented especially from Friday until Sunday. Even the forms of receiving, of hospitality, of our reserve— which has been called "cloistered"—towards secular life should now be in harmony with the urban setting and vocation, and the habitat should be disposed accordingly. As for work and economy, they are neither more nor less difficult to organize in the city than in the country.

The evolution of the city, it is true, presents a new problem to which both the Church and monasticism must seek a solution. It is a fact that most of the urban monasteries are situated in what has become in recent times the heart of the city. Just two examples of these monasteries whose names speak for themselves, Saint-Germain-des-Prés (Saint Germain of the Plains) and Saint-Martin-des-Champs (Saint Martin of the Fields), are no longer situated in the green open spaces, but in the asphalt center of modern Paris. Urban sociology studies show, in light of precise statistics, a phenomenon taking place in the megalopolises of the whole world: the center is becoming depopulated (except for office buildings which are frequented during working days and hours) while the surrounding suburbs are constantly expanding. Consequently, we need two types of urban monasteries, those of the new suburbs and those of the former centers. One of the roles of the latter type would be to favor, through initial encounters, mutual contact, understanding, and reconciliation between two categories of inhabitants of the central district: those who live in luxurious quarters (historical or modern) and the poor who lack the means of emigrating to the new vital centers. I dream of a Commission of Urban Monasticism entrusted with the task of exploring this area. Without doubt, we are moving from rare large communities towards dispersion into small prayer groups, between which there could be a system of relations and exchanges, like that of the Community of Saint Benedict near Paris.

Forms of Realization

There has always been an urban monasticism, but its existence today can no longer be what it was in the past. This is a new type of life in comparison with what it was in the pre-industrial past, and through the grace of the Holy Spirit it is not lacking in the Church. I am thinking of Our Lady of the City Hermitage, situated in the heart of a large metropolis of the United States. There are many instances of the eremitical life but discretion forbids my singling them out until the day a peaceful death reveals the secret, as was the case of Hugette, that Carmelite who, through fidelity to her vocation, left behind her walls and grilles and went to live in an attic in Brussels where I met her and was greatly edified. Her community had enough good sense and charity to support her project and, later on, they provided for her last resting place—their cemetery. Father Poelman has collected some moving memories of her in the review, *La Vie Consacrée.*[4]

Among the new forms of community life, the most well-known in our countries today is that of the monastic community of Saint-Gervais, situated in the heart of Paris. Its members have distributed a short resumé which saves them from having to explain their raison d'être to every visitor. In this brochure they express their plan to create, in the midst of one of the most densely populated quarters, a place of silence and prayer, of hospitality and sharing, of gratuitousness and of peace, where each person is accepted, whatever his condition, his age, his mentality, in that quest for God for whom so many of our contemporaries thirst. It is a beautiful thing to see that such an aspiration can become a reality, not only without conflict with the ancient monastic institutions but with their support.

The group of monks has now been joined by a group of nuns who live not far from them, near the church of Notre-Dame-des-Blanc-Manteaux. The archbishop of Paris has confirmed them in their way of life by writing to them:

> You desire to undertake the contemplative life in the midst of Paris. I am very pleased.
>
> You experience the need for a prolonged period of personal and community prayer along with a daily liturgy. However, you do not wish this liturgy to be lived among you, each and every day, alone or with a small group of select people.
>
> You desire to celebrate the marvels of God's love with the assembly of Christians in a church or a chapel open to all. You do not want to be strangers to the Parisians who come to pray with you.
>
> Finally, your professional work will not only be for you a livelihood but a real participation in the life of the citizens and of the city.
>
> This is an original project and it corresponds to the wishes of the Cardinal to see the creation of centers of prayer adapted to the spiritual needs of the people who live or work in Paris. Thus will you realize your project, humbly, at your place in the Church which is in Paris.
>
> At a time when woman perceives her mission in the world differently than in reference to her situation of wife or mother, the autonomy of your vocation appears as a criterion of authenticity. The dialogue between men and women who pursue the same spiritual experience will be all the more fruitful in the Church if each one brings with him his own particular gifts. In your way, you should work towards the promotion of woman in a society that has not yet given to her her rightful place...

By these facts and this declaration we are now oriented towards the question of knowing to what need urban contemplative communities correspond. What is their purpose?

New Raisons d'Etre

To be realistic, the answer must take into account a distinction between cities in general and, on the other hand, the city of Liège and those that present analogies with it. In all of them, one of the terms used most often to express the role of monasteries is that of an oasis. In the fourth and fifth centuries, the solitudes of Egypt, Syria, and Palestine were so densely populated by hermits and cenobites that they could be compared to veritable cities. An English historian who has written about this phenomenon of the desert becoming a city has affirmed the fact by the very title of his book: *The Desert a City.*[5] Today, in many cases, it is the city which has become a desert because of its immensity and, consequently, because of the impersonal and anonymous relationships between people who pass each other unaware, who live together without communicating. This possibility of living incognito proves to be very favorable to the eremitical vocation. There is no better place to pass without being noticed, to lose oneself in the crowd, to isolate oneself, than the city. However, for those who do not have that vocation, the metropolis has become a place, not of voluntary solitude filled with God, but of resigned isolation, sterile and painful. To remain habitable, such a hell requires compensations in the form of various organizations. There is a proliferation of all kinds of clubs and associations destined to relieve the boredom by games or sports, centers of common interest in business, recreation, and culture. In the religious domain, even the churches, having become so vast and unfavorable to human relations, relieve only a part of the spiritual emptiness from which so many city-dwellers suffer. The role of monasteries is to be extended families which attract, enlighten, warm, and offer to those who desire to come together in God's presence in order to meet him, possibilities that no other institution can furnish.

Their function, then, is both specific and multiple, and the increasing number of Christians who meet together there attests that this service is well fulfilled. What is expected of urban monasteries, and what one effectually finds there, is the testimony and the sharing of that spiritual experience which is union with God realized in prayer. It is contact with the Word of God,

as it is in the Scripture reading they have come to hear and meditate on together; as it is transmitted by a tradition rich with the
doctrine of many saints; as it is received by the members of the
Church who consecrate to it the best part of their time, in order
to be totally penetrated by it and to manifest all the peace, the
joy, and true charity it offers. For prayer, liturgical or other,
accompanied by the background noises of the street, gives to this
meeting with God an extremely realistic character. We do not
distance ourselves from the concrete conditions of the lives of the
men and women of today. We know that we have passed them
on the busy street where they continue their hurried steps and
where we will soon meet them again. We carry within us before
the face of God, invisible and present, all their worries, their
small joys, their suffering, their problems, their interior emptiness, their need of being loved. The love we have just expressed
for God is reflected upon them, and we set out again with
renewed determination to take an interest in them, to smile at
them, to help them too to live by this same love.

This contemplative attitude which overflows into a charitable
activity of indefinite forms cannot be reduced to one of these
benevolent societies specializing in "works of charity." This
attitude requires a living animation and inspiration, a calm
enthusiasm, an unlimited openness to all human distress, which
can only be sustained by the Christian experience in its most
essential, most simple, most profound, most intense, and at the
same time, its most humble element—prayer. Prayer is the action
in which faith becomes explicit, hope receives a constantly
renewed impetus, charity is practiced in the most gratuitous and
disinterested way, that most conformed to the union that existed
between Jesus and his Father in the Holy Spirit, his offering, his
sacrifice, this passage into God's intimacy where he desired, and
continues in his glory to desire, to draw us. Prayer which is
praise, adoration, thanksgiving, informed by the liturgy (but not
exclusively), and whose object is not primarily efficacy. Prayer
which supposes and accepts total renouncement of immediate
results. Who, better than nuns and monks by their consecrated
existence, is prepared for this apparently most futile and yet
most necessary service in the Church?

If they do not accomplish this, allowing themselves to become involved in easier tasks, others will do it in their place; for the Holy Spirit, who inspires so many of our contemporaries with the need of God, does not lack the imagination to raise up from the ground of the Church these centers of resource and of return to the essentials of faith and of it exigencies. In many cities today we see religious institutes (certain of them bear the title of "missionary") reconvert the activities they had adopted in the seventeenth or eighteenth centuries and open "houses of prayer." Sometimes they even move out of the buildings which were only functional in view of their former activities and build new ones especially designed for prayer-oriented activities: rooms for meditation in common, space for adoration, "silent corners," chapels, different rooms for recollection, green spaces according to the possibilities of the site. Recently, during a meeting of experts on religious life, someone asked if active congregations still have a raison d'être. However that may be, there is no doubt that the contemplative orders have a very promising present where they know how to adapt their traditional observances to today's needs.

Motivations and sociological criteria determining the services required can no longer be what they were in the distant past, not even fifty years ago. Monasteries must now become centers of hospitality for both individual lay persons and for lay communities, these ever-more diversified groups that are part of the traditional parish without replacing it or being integrated into it, but bringing to it a necessary complement. They should sometimes be in the parish, and at other times some of them should seek animation and expression in other prayer centers, among these, the monasteries. Certainly, it is difficult for monasteries to adapt themselves to each individual group, nor should they be expected to do so. Each must accept its limitations and make itself available only to particular social groups. It is normal for each monastery to have its own "public," according to its location, be it in the midst of the city, in the suburbs, or in the country; and even in the same district of the city there could be Christian groups of different interests that might come independently or along with other groups. What is important is that for all of them the monastic testimony be authentic and perceptible on two levels or, if you wish, in two areas: that of the quality and the expression of prayer, and that of community life. They should not find just a collectivity, a juxtaposition of individuals—perhaps strongly accentuated individuals, the sum total of which would be just as many individualists—but a community of persons in which each one enriches his own personality by giving and receiving from others in return. A monastery should witness to an authentic community life: first of all on the human level (that of mutual service as in the primitive Church), then on the level of Christian motivations, which are faith, hope, and love, as in the primitive Church. These services and these motives must be perceived by the lay people as valid, but the mutual service and the forms of expressing the motivations should no longer necessarily be—and can no longer be—what they were in the socio-cultural context of the first Christian generations. The Gospel to which monasteries bear witness must remain Good News for today.

NOTES

*First published in *Vie Consacrée*, and in *Prièr dans la Ville*, Paris, 1979. Translated from the French by Sr. Anne-Marie Fitzgerald, OCSO, Abbaye N.-D. de l'Assomption, Rogersville, N.-B., Canada.

1. *The National Institute for Campus Ministries Journal*, vol. 2, no. 2, Spring 1977.

2. Cf. J. Dubois, "Eléments d'une histoire du monachisme urbain," *Lettre de Ligugé*, 143, fasc. 5 (1970), 10-29.

3. H. Atsma, "Les monastères urbains du nord de la Gaule," *Revue d'histoire de l'Eglise de France*, 62 (1976), pp. 165-168, 183-184.

4. R. Poelman, "Une vocation d'érmite," *Vie consacrée*, 48 (1976), pp. 341-351.

5. D.J. Chitty, *The Desert a City*. An Introduction to the Study of Egyptian and Palestinian Monasticism under the Christian Empire, Oxford, 1966.

THE ANGLICAN BENEDICTINES AND RESCUE WORK AMONG THE CITY YOUTH OF ENGLAND

Rene Kollar, OSB
*(St. Vincent Archabbey,
Latrobe, Pennsylvania)*

Monks have traditionally shunned the environs of cities for theological reasons. For some, cities represented the allurements and attractions of a culture which symbolized evil and temptation. *Fuga mundi* meant a flight to a symbolic desert where the monks could work, pray and find salvation liberated from the seductions of an urban society. Pre-Reformation monasteries, therefore, avoided the cities and dotted the desolate forests and fens of England. The Henrician dissolution of the monasteries during the sixteenth century destroyed centuries of English religious traditions, but during the nineteenth century the conventual life began to enjoy popularity within some circles of the Anglican Church. And these new religious communities did not cast disparaging eyes on city life and urban ministry. One young Anglican Benedictine monk, Aelred Carlyle, (1874-1955)[1] tried to reconcile Benedictine monasticism with ministry to the poor and outcast of England's cities, especially the youth.

Despite the anti-monastic legislation of Henry VIII's parliaments and the suspicions of some Englishmen, a current of the monastic ideal continued to flow through some channels of the country's religious life. Little Gidding and the voluntary prayer groups of the Restoration era, for example, kept this tradition alive.[2] Moreover, the heroic examples of priests and religious fleeing to England to escape the horrors of the French Revolution and the emphasis which the Romantic Movement placed on the monastic achievements of the Middle Ages and their contributions to English culture, softened the old mistrust of religious life. The Oxford Movement also discovered the importance of monasticism in the social and political history of the country, and some believed that the conventual life could breathe life into the moribund pastoral and spiritual fiber of nineteenth-century Anglicanism.

Brotherhoods, for example, might invigorate the Anglican parochial system, and several Tractarians spoke to this issue. Hurrell Froude argued that "colleges of unmarried priests would be the cheapest possible way of providing for the spiritual want of a large population."[3] Edward Bouverie Pusey wanted brotherhoods to minister among the poor of England's cities, and believed that Froude's plan was "...the only one, if anything is to be done for our large towns...."[4] John Henry Newman, although he did not write in such a practical manner, also maintained that monastics would protect the Church of England from apathy and indifference.[5] With the exception of Pusey's sisterhood, it fell to the Settlement House Movement later in the century to champion a form of community life based on religious principles which would live and work within an urban environment.

"Toynbee Hall, founded in the slums of London's East End in 1884 by the Reverend Samuel Barnett, was the first settlement house established in England or America and probably remains the best known."[6] According to Standish Meacham, "International competition, industrial obsolescence and technological change, chronic under-employment, and urban decay were forcing social critics and reformers to rethink older attitudes and propose new solutions." The Anglican parochial system had failed to adjust to the new demands of the Victorian slums and the urban working class. One Anglican vicar, for example, noted the "deadness of the Church in so many parishes round, owing in a great measure to the incumbents being broken down...."[7] Another cleric suggested the following solution: "A good country living for the Vicar and a goodly staff of earnest young clerical workers for the parish" in the city.[8] A different response to the obvious problems of the urban poor came from the university town of Oxford.

In November 1883, the Reverend Samuel Barnett presented a paper at St. John's College in which he suggested that university men should undertake communal living in the slums of the capital city to assist the poor. Barnett wanted "to provide education and the means of recreation and enjoyment for the people of the poorer districts of London and the other great cities, to enquire into the conditions of the poor, and to consider and advance plans calculated to promote their welfare."[9] The response was enthusiastic, and in 1884 Toynbee Hall was established in Barnett's parish of St. Jude's located in London's East End district of Whitechapel. Barnett hoped to re-establish a sense of community to heal the class divisions and the unhealthy aspects of the individualism which industrialism had spawned. In addition to rescue work among the youth, "the residents would also cooperate with surrounding clergy, and they would be active in charitable activities, clubs, local government, and university extension teaching."[10]

Barnett based his plans on non-sectarian principles, but soon the Church of England, the Roman Catholic Church, the Salvation Army, and Nonconformists also founded settlements which pitched camp in London's overcrowded areas. The Anglican Church, moreover, enjoyed the valuable contributions of numerous other organizations active in urban missionary work such as the Waifs and Strays Society, White Cross League, and Houses of Mercy, but Anglican officials still continued to search for more effective means to bring the Gospel and social welfare to the poor. The Convocation of Canterbury responded to this need. In April 1888, A. W. Thorold, the Bishop of Rochester, proposed the following resolution in the Upper House of Convocation which called for the appointment of a Committee of both Houses "...to consider and report as to any new organization that might be found to be required for enabling the Church to reach those classes of the population which were now...outside religious ministrations."[11]

The Bishop of Rochester noted that "Christianity was not in possession of South London,"[12] paid special tribute to the important contributions made by the Settlement House movement, but also offered a new twist to the Reverend Barnett's idea. He proposed the establishment "of a new Church brotherhood, to consist of men and women...who should be willing to go and live among the people themselves." The monastic or conventual life, working closely within the existing parochial system, might offer another approach or solution to the problems associated with poverty and unemployment. The debates on this proposal reveal that it enjoyed much support, and on April 25, 1899, the motion passed the Upper House.[13]

A similar resolution introduced in the Lower House by Archdeacon Frederic William Farrar echoed the spirit of its counterpart proposed by the Bishop of Rochester. "The time has come when the Church can...avail herself of the voluntary self-devotion of Brotherhoods, both clerical and lay, the members of which are willing to labor in the service of the Church."[14] Moreover, he pointed out, the working classes "...have become alienated from the ordinances of religion [and]...priceless work might be done among the youth by members of Brotherhoods, trained and set apart for that mission, and more capable of fulfilling it than most of the parochial clergy are or can be."[15] After several months of debate on whether vows were necessary[16] and also affirming the jurisdiction of the local bishop over the brotherhoods, the Lower House adopted a series of resolutions endorsing urban conventual life. The Upper House gave its assent on February 4, 1891. Church of England brotherhoods could now become an important aspect of the church's missionary efforts in the country's cities, and idealistic Anglicans such as Aelred Carlyle began to dream.

By 1896, the twenty-two year-old Benjamin Carlyle, who had adopted the name "Aelred" three years earlier to signify his devotion to monastic ideals, had abandoned studies as a medical student and become a Benedictine oblate associated with the Anglican nuns at West Malling, Kent. In March of that year, he received some financial backing from his mother and bought a small house on the Isle of Dogs in London's East End, and he christened the dwelling which was situated in St. John's parish, "The Priory." He had come to the Isle of Dogs with a preliminary outline of the brotherhood he hoped to establish there. Based broadly on the writings of the French Benedictine, Jean Baptiste Muard, his personal impressions gathered during visits to the Roman Catholic monastery of Buckfast, and research during his oblate period, Carlyle reconciled the peaceful detachment of a contemplative with the social zeal of a missionary.

To combat urban poverty, Carlyle proposed the establishment of brotherhoods or monastic houses in the midst of slums.
The Rule of St. Benedict provided the basis, and the monks
would pray according to the Benedictine breviary in English.
While not condemning the affairs of the world, he did argue,
however, that if evil existed, the church had a duty to correct it:
"God so loved the world that He of old devised a plan to save it,
and it is to the *entire* world and not to any mere section of it that
the love of God sets forth today, and so until the entire world has
been conquered, God's entire will had not been carried out."[17]
Vice and complacency could be found throughout English
society, and both the Church of England and Parliament continued to approach the problems of society with a sense of smug
satisfaction. In the brotherhoods, however, his monks would
"live like a shining example of a Christ-like Christian, a living
witness to the truths of his belief."[18]

Carlyle's early blueprint for Anglican monasticism would
accommodate three varieties or types of monks. The first, the
contemplatives, would reside in the country and follow a strict
interpretation of the Benedictine Rule. Their work would include
preaching, caring for the needs of society's outcasts, and possibly
running a rescue house for youth. The active monks, on the other
hand, would work exclusively among the urban poor and a
"missionary vow" would signify this commitment. "The chief
object of their lives," Carlyle's plan stated, "is to preach, hold
missions, care for the sick and fulfill the thousand obligations of
a perfect missionary."[19] Moreover, it "...is to live in the midst of
ungodliness, of poverty and misery indescribable, that God calls
him [the active monk] to settle." Finally the so-called "secular
monks" would also reside in the poorer areas of the cities, but
their activity would not be strictly religious in nature. They
would labor among the poor as "lawyers, doctors, businessmen,
clerks working each in his daily profession, a zealous missionary
showing to his companions the true religion of Christ by his
integrity of life, his purity, and his unswerving and manly faith
in God."[20]

The demands of parish life on the Isle of Dogs, however,
forced Carlyle to modify the monastic flavor behind his plans.
He did retain the externals of the monastic life, for example, he

styled himself as a Benedictine prior and wore a religious habit throughout the parish, but social work occupied the majority of his time and energy. Within a year he realized that his life at St. John's was "a basis of activity, work, missions, etc., very little rules and regulations supplemented by periods of regular retirement to the less active house for spiritual refreshment."[21] His chief concern had become "the poor boys of the slums."[22] Carlyle taught catechism to the youth of the parish on Saturdays, and in the evenings he entertained the local boys at the priory "where the working lads and young men...came just for talking and smoking."[23] Frustrated, Carlyle left London in February 1898.

For the next four years, Aelred Carlyle moved throughout England and Wales looking for a favorable spot to experiment with his dreams for Anglican monasticism. He also began to attract some attention and support from church authorities. In the Spring of 1898, the Archbishop of Canterbury, Frederick Temple, authorized his solemn profession as an Anglican Benedictine monk and in March 1902, Carlyle and several companions accepted the invitation of Lord Halifax and moved to his Yorkshire estate at Painsthorpe. Within a year, the American Bishop of Fond du Lac, Charles Grafton, blessed him as an Anglican Benedictine Abbot. This patronage and stability gave Carlyle the opportunity to experiment again with a monastic house engaged in urban missionary work. At the invitation of the Rev. C. N. Long, Vicar of St. Aidan's in Birmingham, Carlyle dispatched one of his monks, Bro. Austin Green, to explore the possibilities of opening a rescue house for boys in this Midland city in August 1904.

The *Church Times* welcomed the interest of these Anglican Benedictines in the needs of the city, and reported the progress of this new foundation. According to the paper, "...one of the brethren recently arrived in Birmingham to fix upon a congenial spot for the inauguration of an effort to reach the waifs and strays of the city by gathering them into homes where... neglected boys will be assisted to become good Churchmen, and of necessity good citizens also."[24] "He contends that boys thrown upon the streets," the *Church Times* continued, "often have no chance of rising above their surroundings unless...they do something which causes them to fall into the hands of the police." England's reformatories and institutions had failed: individualism and character suffered; and religious instruction amounted "to little more than undenominational-ism." Bro. Austin's initial response was enthusiastic. "Church life in Birmingham," he noticed, "seems of late to have received fresh impetus, and to be entering on a new lease of activity."[25]

Moreover, Bro. Austin told the newspaper that the monastic spirit had something more to offer than cold, efficient bureaucracy, namely, the idea of community or family living. "It is proposed therefore to begin with six lads, and gradually raise the number to twenty, when a new house will be started," he pointed out, and suggested that two "brothers will be in charge of the home, the idea being to lead a family life with the boys." Envisioning a network of these homes in the future, Bro. Austin believed that they should eventually become self-supporting. The boys would receive their education at the neighborhood elementary school and the brothers would assist them in finding jobs after their schooling. But, he emphasized, St. Benet's Home, the first home, would not be another trade school; Christian principles would form an essential part of the spirit of St. Benet's.

Bro. Austin returned to Painsthorpe and reported his impressions to Aelred Carlyle, who shared the same excitement about the project. The September 1904 edition of *Pax*, the community newsletter published by the Yorkshire Benedictine community which now numbered seventeen, announced the establishment of St. Benet's Home for Boys associated with St. Aidan's parish in Birmingham. Abbot Carlyle reminded the readers that the "Community has always had in view the development of Active Work as an extension and complement of the Religious Life."[26] While emphasizing the contemplative life, Carlyle stressed the fact that this "interior work" did not necessarily rule out "exterior" or active work and Birmingham would become this new vineyard. He asked people to support this "...useful work among the poor little destitute lads of Birmingham,"[27] and stressed that this endeavor was not inconsistent with the history of his Anglican Benedictines. "In opening this House," Carlyle wrote,

I would make it quite clear to our readers that we do not seek to emulate or to criticise any existing organization which exists for the same good purpose. There are several such in Birmingham doing noble work; but the need is so great in our large centres of population, that it would be very difficult indeed to have too many such Homes, and I do feel that there is a place for ours, and this feeling is endorsed by the support Birmingham is already giving to us.[28]

A specifically monastic spirit, moreover, would color this project. "The Brothers will live among the boys, and our chief aim, which I wish to emphasise, is to try to make a real family of each household; and for this reason we do not intend to increase the number of boys in each house to more than twenty...." The concept of community or family, which Carlyle had stressed in his earlier writings, appeared again. "Those we want are the little heathen lads of our great cities whose houses have never been homes to them; whose little lives have been almost animal in their limitations; and who have never known the love of father or mother, or the healthy affection of decent friends." Abbot Carlyle's settlement, therefore, would take these young lads "From their surroundings while they are young, feed them, clothe them, educate them, and, above all, teach them that they have a work to do for God in His world...."

Carlyle supplied the philosophy behind St. Benet's Home for Boys, but Bro. Austin held the responsibility for the establishment of the home and was in charge of its daily operations. He rented a small dwelling in the Small Heath district of Birmingham for a yearly rent of £22 and quickly began to remodel the dwelling to accommodate the new borders. A brochure told the public that the home would "...give to poor and friendless boys all the associations of a happy home life, and at the same time training to take their place in the future as instructed citizens and useful citizens."[29] And Bro. Austin made it clear that the "class of boy we want to receive is the very poorest, the homeless, and friendless, *before they have been convicted*."[30] Free gifts of clothes, furnishings, and food[31] made the dwelling welcoming for the first lads who arrived on September 25, 1904.

Bro. Austin drew up a strict and exacting schedule for St. Benet's. He would accept boys between the ages of ten and thirteen, and he recognized that his first duty "...will be to get them clean and tidy, and then to see to their proper education."[32] These lads would attend the local council school. Sports and games also occupied a special place in the routine, but one could also recognize the monastic atmosphere of St. Benet's. "The whole Family will meet every morning for Prayers and Catechism, and the evenings will be spent in games, home lessons, etc., and will end with Compline. The attic will make a very nice Oratory. The housework will be done among us."

Hoping to develop "a strong healthy, manly character," he listed the qualities which he wanted to stress. Bro. Austin set a limit of twenty boys to each house to accentuate the ideal of "Family Life." Moreover, the "Brother-in-charge will in every way share the daily life of the boys and live with them as an elder brother." A criminal record eliminated anyone from consideration. The boys would be encouraged to think of St. Benet's as their home, and even after their education and training they would be invited to remain in residence for a time. Anglo-Catholic devotions and practices, moreover, would form a "well-instructed Churchman, and therefore...an honourable citizen." Finally, Bro. Austin never let anyone forget that the Anglican Benedictine community at Painsthorpe sponsored this mission in Birmingham.

Little information has survived about the number of boys who entered under Bro. Austin's care or the early progress of the house. Aelred Carlyle journeyed to St. Benet's at least twice, and he appeared pleased at the progress. At a visit during the autumn of 1904, Carlyle reported that he found "a most united and happy little family at the Home and Brother Austin and I had a long talk about ways and means."[33] Moreover, Carlyle released Bro. Austin from all duties and obligations to the Yorkshire community in order that a full-time commitment could be given to the Birmingham mission. Carlyle also asked the readers of *Pax* to support the endeavor with prayers and financial gifts. Bro. Austin also worked well with the Vicar of St. Aidan's parish and the Bishops of Worcester, Charles Gore and H. W. Yeatman-Biggs. He did, however, experience difficult times. From the beginning, Bro. Austin had to beg for money, food, clothing, and material for the small oratory. Despite these efforts, this early experiment in urban monastic rescue work did not succeed.

Suffering with pneumonia for nearly six months, Bro. Austin Green died on Sunday evening February 11, 1906. The obituary gave a brief biographical sketch, but devoted more space to his association with St. Benet's Home for Boys.[34] He leaves "a home fatherless in no ordinary sense of the word," the *Church Times* noted, "as well as a host of friends with an aching sense as of a light gone out of their lives." The paper stressed the fact that Bro. Austin arrived in Birmingham penniless, but "full of a longing to make a home for homeless boys." His success among the youth of the city was recognized, and several individuals paid public tribute to his work at St. Benet's.[35] His death, consequently, deprived the home of effective leadership and also revealed its financial weakness. When Bro. Austin died, the *Church Times* reported that £50 was needed immediately to keep the house open, and an appeal drive was immediately launched by interested members of the city. But Abbot Carlyle's interest in city missionary work also began to wane.

Ordained a priest in 1904 by Bishop Charles Grafton of Fond du Lac, Carlyle began to devote more time and effort to the welfare of his monastic community and his position within the Anglican Church. In July 1906, he moved his community from Yorkshire to Caldey Island, South Wales, and this isolation meant a physical detachment from the problems and concerns of the cities. Moreover, Carlyle's vision of Anglican monasticism had become more contemplative, and this change appeared in "Our Purpose, Method, and Rule," originally published in 1907. While not berating the so-called "active life" of pastoral ministry, Carlyle pointed out that it "would be obviously wrong...for him who has received certain gifts and attractions for work which would lie among the sinful, the sick and the outcast, or for the education of the young to seek to live under a Rule like that of St. Benedict which sets before its disciples as its *primary* end the recitation of the Divine Office, and the actions of the Contemplative Life."[36] But the events of Carlyle's life would bring him full circle to his youthful attraction to a ministry of active social work In 1913, he and the majority of the Caldey community converted to Roman Catholicism. Eight years later Carlyle resigned as Abbot, and spent approximately thirty-three years in British Columbia where he distinguished himself as a missionary to the Indians, a prison and port chaplain, and with work in a home for the aged. Carlyle eventually returned to England and died on October 14, 1955.

NOTES

1. For biographies of Aelred Carlyle and his attempts to establish Benedictine monasticism in the Church of England, see: P. Anson, *Abbot Extraordinary. A Memoir of Aelred Carlyle, Monk and Missionary, 1874-1955* (London: The Faith Press, 1958); and R. Kollar, "Abbot Aelred Carlyle and the Monks of Caldey: Anglo-Catholicism in the Church of England, 1895-1913" (Ph.D. diss., University of Maryland, 1981).

2. See the following for history of religious and conventual life in the Anglican Church: A.M. Allchin, *The Silent Revolution: Anglican Religious Communities, 1846-1900* (London: SCM Press, 1958); and P. Anson, *The Call of the Cloister. Religious Communities and Kindred Bodies in the Anglican Communion* (London: SPCK, 1964). The latter also contains a fine, but outdated, bibliography.

3. Quoted in L. Guiney, *Hurrell Froude* (London: Methuen, 1904), 122.

4. Quoted in H. Liddon, *Life of Edward Bouverie Pusey*, vol. 2, (London: Longmans, Green Co., 1893), 38.

5. H. Newman, *Historical Sketches*, vol. 2, (London: Longmans, Green Co., 1906), 102. Newman argued here that if anyone studied the monastic tradition "...he will see how much was gained to Christianity in purity; as well as unity, by that monastic system."

6. S. Meacham, *Toynbee Hall and Social Reform 1880-1914. The Search for Community* (New Haven: Yale University Press, 1987), ix.

7. Quoted in H. McLeod, *Class and Religion in the Late Victorian City* (Hamden, CT: Archon Books, 1974), 105.

8. *Ibid*. For other descriptions of the plight of the urban poor and the failure of the Anglican Church to meet these conditions, see also: D. Bowen, *The Idea of the Victorian Church* (Montreal: McGill University Press, 1968); O. Chadwick, *The Victorian Church*, Part II (London: A.C. Black, 1971); L. Elliott-Binns, *Religion and the Victorian Era* (London: The Lutterworth Press, 1936); and K.S. Inglis, *Churches and the Working Class in Victorian England* (London: Routledge and Kegan Paul, 1974).

9. H.O. Barnett, *Canon Barnett. His Life, Work and Friends* (London: J. Murray, 1908), 311.

10. K.S. Inglis, *Churches and the Working Class in Victorian England*, 146.

11. *Chronicle of Convocation. Upper House, 1899* (London: National Society's Repository, 1905), 109.

12. *Ibid.*, 210.

13. *Ibid.*, 112.

14. *Chronicle of Convocation, Lower House, 1899*, 235.

15. *Ibid.*, 239.

16. The resolution of the Lower House contained the words *vows* and *dispensation*, but the Upper House eliminated these and substituted instead "lifelong engagement to the life and work of the community." Moreover, the local bishop could "release" a member from these obligations.

17. A. Carlyle, "The English Order of St. Benedict: Future," Prinknash Abbey Archives, Prinknash Abbey, Cranham, Gloucester, 16.

18. *Ibid.*, 17.

19. *Ibid.*, 11.

20. *Ibid.*, 19.

21. A. Carlyle to D. Cowan [Vicar of St. John's Parish], 1 June 1897, Archbishop Davidson Papers, Caldey, Lambeth Palace Library, Lambeth Palace, London.

22. A. Carlyle, Diary, Autumn 1948, Prinknash Abbey Archives.

23. H. Watts to M. Hanbury, 15 December 1959, Prinknash Abbey Archives. Watts was one of Carlyle's companions on the Isle of Dogs.

24. *Church Times* (London), 26 August 1904.

25. "St. Benet's Home for Boys, Birmingham," *Pax*, September 1904, 15.

26. *Ibid.*, 14.

27. A. Carlyle, "Community Letter," *Pax*, September 1904, 22.

28. *Ibid.*

29. "St. Mark's and St. Benet's Home for Boys," 1904, Prinknash Abbey Archives. Soon after the establishment of St. Benet's, Bro. Austin joined forces with another small home, St. Mark's, founded earlier by an Anglican cleric, the Rev. James Adderley.

30. Bro. Austin, "St. Benet's Home for Boys, Birmingham," *Pax*, September 1904, 16.

31. Bro. Austin, "St. Benet's Home for Boys, Birmingham," *Pax*, December 1904, 47.

32. See note 30 above.

33. A. Carlyle, "Community Letter," *Pax*, December 1904, 47.

34. *Church Times,* 16 February 1906.

35. *Church Times,* 16 February 1906; *Church Times,* 23 February 1906; *Church Times,* 23 March 1906.

36. A. Carlyle, "Our Purpose, Method, and Rule" in W.R. Shepherd, ed., *The Benedictines of Caldey Island* (Isle of Caldey: The Abbey, 1912), 83.

THE MONASTERY AS CITY—
ITS ROLE IN THE EVANGELIZATION
OF THE CHURCH

Archabbot Notker Wolf, OSB
(Abbey of St. Ottilien, Germany)

On January 2, 1994, the monks of Hanga in Tanzania elected their first African abbot. The monastery had been raised to an abbey on December 13 of the previous year, which is the feast day of St. Ottilia, the patron saint of the Benedictine Congregation of St. Ottilien. Two weeks after his election, Abbot Alcuin Nyirenda received the abbatial blessing from Norbert Mtega, the local archbishop. It was a major event for the population, the local church and the whole Church of Tanzania. Bishops, priests, sisters and many people joined in the colorful celebration. It was also an important step for the Benedictine Congregation of St. Ottilien, 110 years after its beginning and 106 years after the arrival of the first missionary monks of St. Ottilien in the country. The solemn occasion was marked by the presence of abbots and priors from monasteries in all parts of the world.

1. From Solitude to a Monastic City: An African Example

Hanga was started in the late '50s as an exclusively African community. The Africans were to develop their own lifestyle, and Liganga, where the foundation began, was conceived as a community of a more contemplative character than its "motherhouse" of Peramiho. They were meant to keep alive the monastic charism even after the departure of the missionaries which then was presumed imminent due to the African independence movements.[1]

The first African superior moved the foundation to Hanga which was, at that time, a very solitary place. Nowadays about 8000 people are living in the village around the monastery. They have settled there because of the monastery, although the exact reasons might not be very clear to the people themselves. It seems that they were attracted by the monastery and feel secure living in its shadow. This emerging village has completely altered the lifestyle of the monks. They were looking for solitude but since people have come they feel obliged to look after those who are poor in a material or spiritual sense. Sharing, after all, is a basic principle in African tradition.

After some years, people followed the example of the monks by growing corn which had previously been thought impossible in that region. In this they were helped and encouraged by the monks.[2] The monks also had to open a parish which was then handed over to the bishop, although the bishop would have preferred it to be run by the monks. The monastery initiated several projects, including a soccer team.

The impact of the Benedictine community on the population is amazing; the whole monastery has developed according to the needs of the people. Many years ago they started a minor seminary for aspirants to any kind of religious life in Tanzania, because the minor seminaries were full with vocations to the secular priesthood and did not really foster the spirit of religious charisms. First Hanga set up this school for its own purposes, but soon other religious orders applied. For some years this school was ranked second among the country's private schools, but people from the region also hankered after education. As teachers were available, the monks started a day school for boys and girls from the surrounding area which today numbers 200 students. A small pharmacy has recently been replaced by a dispensary with ten rooms and several beds for emergency treatment. There are apprentices being trained in various crafts in the workshops of the monastery. The monks, who were looking for more water for the monastery, simultaneously provided three villages with sufficient clean water. Hanga has not only developed into an abbey with its liturgy and regular monastic schedule, but also turned out to be a spiritual and cultural center for the whole region.

There is no wall around the buildings, but the core of the monastery—church, regular rooms and living quarters—is closed in a rectangular form. The other buildings are nearby and form a larger unit which is surrounded by a natural fence of bushes and trees. The village itself touches the monastery only from one side.

It is hardly surprising, then, that other bishops have asked the monks for new foundations. Mvimwa, in the diocese of Sumbawanga, in the western part of Tanzania, started in 1979 and will become an independent priory by Pentecost of 1995. Another foundation was begun a few years ago in Katibunga, in the neighboring country of Zambia. In Kipalapala, in the archdiocese of Tabora, the monks have taken over responsibility for the printing press of the Tanzanian Episcopal Conference. The community was raised to a simple priory in 1992. There are two more dependent houses and also two farms. There are altogether 89 monks in solemn vows, 47 in temporary vows, and 9 novices. Twenty miles away, in a remote formation house in the bush, those boys who are interested in monastic life are being trained and scrutinized.

These new foundations go through the same process as the motherhouse, Hanga. Mvimwa, too, began far away from any major settlement. Its founder, Fr. Gregory Mwageni, the first conventual prior of Hanga, also had been looking for extreme solitude. But soon the chapel became too small on Sundays, the monks had to start some kind of dispensary, and boys are now being trained in the workshops and on the farm. The only resident priest was asked by the bishop to give retreats for priests and sisters. The influence of the monastery on the area has grown remarkably. Perhaps one of the most visible proofs is this: When the monks started, there were hardly any fields to be seen. The local population consisted chiefly of hunters and fruit-pickers. Six years later, many fields of corn and wheat covered the region. Meanwhile the local people have also imitated the monks by planting trees.[3] Katibunga in Zambia is undergoing a similar development.

At Kipalapala the first group arrived in order to receive some training on the printing press. They established a small community and were soon joined by some local boys who came and asked to live like the monks. These boys got their first formation there and later were sent to Hanga. After the White Fathers gave up the press, the community, and the people of Hanga itself, felt that they could not abandon the bishops and their printing press and so the monks remained and started a new monastery. The management of the printing press of the Bishops' Conference is an important contribution to the work of evangelization in the local church. A monastic community guarantees continual assistance to that project, while on the other hand such an activity fosters the unity of a community, keeps the monks together, and does not disturb their monastic schedule.

These young monasteries have developed into spiritual and cultural centers by a natural process. They intended to be very Benedictine but—because of the sociological and cultural context in which they found themselves—turned into monasteries of the kind which flourished during the early Middle Ages, when Europe's evangelization was fostered and supported by the famous abbeys of St. Gall, Reichenau, Fulda and others.[4] They are developing into small cities, and are becoming centers of evangelization and development.

As such they are perhaps more efficient than many of the state-sponsored development projects in Third World Countries. They are not implanted from outside; they are rooted in the mentality of the local people and grow in an organic way. Simultaneously a monastic community guarantees the continuity of these kinds of development projects. And so the monastery is influenced by the surrounding environment, and the people living around it are influenced by the life of the community.

There are several other new communities of the Congregation of St. Ottilien which show similar developments, such as Tigoni-Nairobi in Kenya, Tororo in Uganda, Agbang in Togo, Digos on Mindanao Island, Philippines, and Kumily in India. These monasteries are models of Christian inculturation in its full sense.

2. Evangelization by Monasteries—An Idea of the Benedictine Revival of the Nineteenth Century

2.1. *The origin of the idea*

This contemporary development in these monasteries is a realization of an idea by Fr. Andreas Amrhein, who founded the monastery and the Congregation of St. Ottilien in 1884. During his theological studies in Tübingen, he came in contact with Professor (later Bishop) Hefele whose appraisal of the monastic contribution to the christianization and civilization of Europe deeply impressed Amrhein. During this period, Amrhein also studied the diaries of David Livingstone, the famous explorer of Africa and an Anglican missionary. In one of his reflections, Livingstone blamed the Lutheran missionaries for baptizing only the brain but not the whole body. In his view they should imitate the medieval Benedictines in England who had transformed the whole human being or, as we would say nowadays, who had evangelized the whole culture of the people.

Amrhein consequently joined the abbey of Beuron in order to become a Benedictine monk, but in his mind the idea of starting a new monastery which would take up the old missionary tradition of the monks had already taken root. He was determined that in his era of new missionary enterprise and of growing colonialism, the monastic and Benedictine charism should bear its share of the missionary effort. The Benedictines were called once again to provide stability in a world which was quickly changing in a period of great migrations.[5]

2.2. Missionary monasteries in Eastern and Southern Africa

Soon after the foundation of St. Ottilien—which simultaneously was also the cradle of the Tutzing Missionary Benedictine Sisters—the first group consisting of one priest, nine brothers and four sisters, was sent out to East Africa, which was then under German colonial administration. In 1888 they started a double-monastery for sisters and monks in Pugu, near Daressalaam.[6] The first thing they did after their arrival was to hang a bell in a tree and to sing Latin Vespers. Within a few months the building of the entire monastery was completed.[7] It did not last long, however. One year later it was burnt down in the course of an indigenous revolt and two brothers and one sister were killed, and three brothers and one sister were taken captive for several weeks. Others had already died of diseases. They soon started to build another monastery, this time in Daressalaam: St. Joseph's for the monks, St. Mary's for the sisters. They soon realized that there was no possibility of getting local vocations unless they first established a Christian environment by preaching, setting up mission stations, schools and hospitals, and, at a later date, printing presses and shops. In order to preserve the Benedictine tradition of the Middle Ages, they planned large stations, with several monks, as priories and smaller stations as monastic cells.[8]

A long and fruitful mission period started. The Benedictine missionary method, however, had to be partially modified under the pressure of circumstances: Two world wars and the great massive desire for baptism among the African population did not allow for the establishment of large priories. But for most of the time there were two or three monks at any one station, priest-monks and lay-brothers. They recited their morning and evening office in common, had their meals together with reading and had communal recreation. The sisters lived together in their own convents.

Whereas in the beginning the whole southern half of modern Tanzania had been entrusted to the Benedictines, they had to confine their work to a smaller southern part of the country after the First World War. It stretched from the Indian Ocean to Lake Nyassa. The original Benedictine mission territory has meanwhile developed into eleven dioceses in two ecclesiastical provinces.

The remaining vast southern part was erected as the territory of the *abbatia nullius* Lindi which, in 1932, was split into two *abbatiae nullius*, Peramiho and Ndanda. They remained the chief monastic and ecclesiastical centers until the gradual creation of a local hierarchy in six dioceses under the metropolitan of Songea. These two abbeys provided a home for the missionaries living on the many distant outstations, and they also sheltered two large convents of the Tutzing Missionary Benedictine Sisters. These monasteries were also responsible (and to a certain extent still are) for various educational establishments in the area: Peramiho founded a philosophical-theological faculty which today serves five dioceses, a teachers' training college, secondary schools for boys and girls, elementary schools, a nursing school, and a trade school. Ndanda likewise established secondary and elementary schools, nursing and trade schools and, for some time, also has had an agricultural school. Each monastery runs a printing press and a publishing house. They take care of two major hospitals and are partially responsible for a few hospitals at the main missions, not to mention the numerous dependent dispensaries. Many people have settled around these monasteries. The parish of Peramiho for example currently comprises 32,000 Catholics.[9]

After the local church had been erected and most of the mission stations had been transformed into ordinary parishes entrusted to secular priests, the role of these monasteries in evangelization changed. During the first hundred years their prime task was to preach the gospel and to implant the Church in the country. They were the temporal and spiritual centers for the missionary work. Even though the missionaries often were away from the monasteries for most of the year, they knew that the abbeys were their monastic homes. At the same time they maintained their basic stability in the European monasteries of their profession, to which they returned for home-leave—in the first decades once every ten or twenty years—or in their old age because of ill health. They were assigned to the mission monasteries but they rarely transferred their stability. Nevertheless, because of the unique situation of the mission monasteries, the monks elected the abbot in the monasteries to which they had been assigned.

Nowadays most of the parishes have been handed over to the bishops. The abbeys are providing only a few parish priests, and these are generally monks who have spent most of their lives in such responsibilities. The communities have learned that during this period of transition they must assume new functions in the local churches. Whereas previously they had expected to close down once their missionary task was fulfilled, they now hope to continue to contribute to the spiritual development of their local church. This is needed even more if the faith is to take firm root. They have now started to build retreat houses and to preach retreats for priests, sisters and lay people.

After the communities had decided to remain in the country it became obvious that they would have to accept native vocations in order to become true local communities. The lack of new vocations from overseas hastened this decision. But it is a rather difficult ideal. The Europeans have built up a way of life which does not really meet the African way.[10] Still, they are giving it a try and both abbeys hope to succeed.

It is striking to observe that the monastery of Hanga, which never intended to take over the European monastery of Peramiho with its many institutions, is developing along the same lines, becoming an evangelizing city, whereas Peramiho is adopting the ways of Hanga. Both have become "monastic and evangelizing cities," one intentionally so from the outset, the other through the force of its ecclesial and social context. Ndanda, too, is developing in similar fashion.

The same model of intentional "evangelization by monastic cities" has been realized in other monasteries like Inkamana in South Africa with its famous high school for black boys and girls. For a long time it has enabled the black population to take on greater responsibilities, and we shall see the results of this training now after South Africa has found a peaceful way of integration. After graduation, most of the black students were able to go on to universities. They are going to play an important role in the new society.

2.3. Missionary monasteries in Asia

The Abbey of Waegwan in South Korea, too, has found its role in the South Korean Church. The monks—Germans and Koreans—have translated the New Testament, with a commentary, which has become an official version recognized by the Bishops' Conference. Their printing press and audio-visual center enjoy a high reputation even outside the Church. Some of the monks are in charge of the national correspondence course for catechumens which has been initiated by the Bishops' Conference. Others have played an important role in the democratization movement, the farmers' movement and also in the workers' social rights development. A retired former abbot is still organizing prayer meetings for the evangelization of North Korea in the name of the Bishops' Conference.

When the Congregation of St. Ottilien arrived in Seoul in 1909, the monks intended to build a regular monastery with schools, and this monastery in 1913 became the second abbey within the Congregation, one year before the first foundations of St. Ottilien in Germany, Münsterschwarzach and Schweiklberg, were raised to abbeys and St. Ottilien to an archabbey. The

Japanese domination of Korea since 1910 made it impossible for the monks to continue with their schools. The Japanese intended to japanize Korea completely and to suppress Korean culture. Therefore in 1920, the Congregation for the Propagation of the Faith entrusted the eastern third of North Korea to the monks as their new mission territory, together with the eastern half of Manchuria. The abbey of Seoul was transferred to Tokwon in North Korea where the monks established a famous philosophical-theological seminary. Several bishops and many priests who worked in South Korea after the end of the Korean War in 1953 had originally been trained by the Benedictines of Tokwon. Tokwon was also renowned for its agriculture, and the communists have continued that tradition up to the present: today the former abbey buildings house the agricultural faculty of the University of Wonsan.[11]

In 1985, contacts were resumed with the former mission area of Yenki (now Yanji) in Manchuria, the northeast of China. The Benedictines had established an abbey in Yanji in 1934. In 1946 a diocese was erected there. The monastery had set up a printing press which produced translations of spiritual texts and school books, ran a trade school, some of whose former pupils are still alive and are among the most faithful Christians there. The Olivetan Sisters of Cham in Switzerland cooperated in the schools and a small hospital. Still now, after forty years, the influence of the former monastery can be noted. Among the large Chinese population the Christians are only a small minority, and yet they provide a good base for a new launching of evangelization. Many, especially among the priests, are waiting for a reestablishment of the monastery which the present political regulations do not allow.[12]

3. The Evangelizing Dimension of Benedictine Monasteries

Similar examples could easily be recounted from other monasteries around the world. The same story could be told about the abbeys of Münsterschwarzach, Schweiklberg and Königsmünster in Germany. They were originally founded as centers for the training of missionary monks and to raise funds for missionary work. Together with a monastery in Switzerland

and three houses in the Americas they have contributed to the support of missionary activities throughout the first part of this century. In a spirit of solidarity, they continue to assist the young churches and their monasteries. At the same time, their minor seminaries have been transformed into open schools, they have introduced extensive programs of religious formation, and two of these houses are running modern printing presses which produce theological and spiritual books. These communities are no longer oriented exclusively towards the overseas missions but have discovered a new evangelizing role in their own backyards.

Maybe it is because of this openness of the local people and the local church that even the young foundations in Africa and Asia, which were started around or after Vatican II, have taken the same direction although they never had any particular intention of growing into such multi-faceted monastic forms. Thus also the older monasteries have not lost their function, in spite of the crisis of missionary fervor after the colonial era and the Vatican Council. The new concept of mission makes it essentially a charism of the whole Church, not just of some missionary congregations, but this did not affect the original idea of the monastic community as a spiritual and cultural center of evangelization. Besides all kind of activities, the basic missionary "work" is the witness of a Christian community, the living and celebrating and working together, where God is the center of their life and his love towards man is continued in the service to the people.

This opens the view to the general evangelizing dimension of Benedictine monasticism. When Boniface Wimmer, from the Bavarian abbey of Metten, and Martin Marty, from Engelberg in Switzerland, went to North America in order to found monastic communities, the medieval pattern had been their incentive. These monasteries were conceived as stable centers of reference for the immigrants and so developed agriculture, built schools and major seminaries, took over the pastoral care of neighboring communities and began missionary work among the Indians.[13] These monasteries have grown into large monastery-cities and, together with the Benedictine Sisters, have played an important role in the development of the Catholic Church in the United States.

In present day Europe contemplative monasteries are attracting many Christians who are in search of spiritual renewal or who wish to strengthen their faith. English, Swiss, Bavarian and Austrian monasteries are continuing their ancient tradition of providing higher education. Most have been looking after parishes for many centuries.

For some decades there has been a prolonged discussion on whether Benedictine monasteries should be involved in the missionary work of the Church. During the Benedictine renewal of the last century there was a strong tendency towards a narrowly contemplative definition of the Benedictine way of life. Monks were supposed to live their life within the wall of the enclosure. They should not get involved in pastoral or missionary commitments.

This ideal caused the Tutzing Missionary Benedictine Sisters to adopt the structure of modern congregations and to set up priories rather than abbeys, unlike their brothers in the Congregation of St. Ottilien who were allowed to take up the traditional structure and in 1904 became members of the Benedictine Confederation. Only in female monasteries like St. Walburg in Eichstätt and Frauenchiemsee, which were founded in the early Middle Ages before papal enclosure was introduced, were the nuns allowed to continue their tradition and to leave the enclosure in order to teach in the schools.

Chapter 66 of the Rule of St. Benedict says: "The monastery should, if possible, be so constructed that within it all necessities, such as water, mill, and garden, are contained, and the various crafts are practiced. Then there will be no need for the monks to roam outside, because this is not at all good for their souls." This might be interpreted in the strict sense that monks should not have activities outside the enclosure. But does this really prevent monks from going out to preach the gospel, building up a local church? We have to bear in mind the reason St. Benedict gives for his advice: "not to roam around outside." This is a matter of discipline and must not be confused with a fulfillment of the evangelical command of spreading the good news and baptizing. History shows that, besides monks who were prominent missionary pioneers, it was the monasteries which became influential places of evangelization where people flocked for spiritual and cultural education. Important pastoral tasks were fulfilled from within the enclosure. The community as *ecclesiola* has done this important work within the Church. The Benedictine monastery, which originally had not been conceived of as a missionary institution, has turned out to be an efficient means among other kinds of evangelization methods. This holds true not only for Benedictine monasticism, but also for the orthodox monks and monasteries in Greece and Eastern Europe, for the evangelization of Egypt, Ethiopia and Kerala, even beyond Christianity, where for example the Buddhist religion in Asia was spread by monks.

On the other hand there have been different developments at different times. The *Dialogues* of St. Gregory the Great show that St. Benedict preached the Gospel when he first arrived at Montecassino. Later he withdrew completely into the monastery. When the first monks arrived in Tanzania they felt the need of preaching the Gospel and baptizing people. It is only now, after the local church has been implanted, that the monks withdraw from the parishes and see their major contribution in the development of their monastic centers which all these years have supported and completed the evangelization of the people.

That means that the Benedictine life in various ways has its missionary vocation within the universal mission of the Church. Not all the monasteries have developed into the manifold structure of this kind of monastic city, but the different vocations have produced different developments and continue to do this in our day in many new foundations all over the world.

There is, however, one important difference: monastic cities like the city of St. Gall, where the abbot was simultaneously a secular prince, no longer have a place in our world. Feudalism is over. But that does not prevent people from settling again in the vicinity of a monastery. History does not repeat itself, but similar intentions in similar circumstances may lead to similar solutions. Monasteries as praying and working communities will always attract people, or rather: God attracts and brings them close to the Church, thus transforming the people and the Church herself.[14]

Further reading on modern Benedictine missions:

B. Doppelfeld, Mönchtum und kirchlicher Heilsdienst. Entstehung und Entwicklung des nordamerikanischen Benediktinertums im 19. Jahrhundert (Münsterschwarzacher Studien vol. 22), Münsterschwarzach, 1974.

F. Renner, (ed.), Der fünfarmige Leuchter. Beiträge zum Werden und Wirken der Benediktinerkongregation von St. Ottilien, 4 vols. St. Ottilien, 1971-1993.

G. Sieber, The Benedictine Congregation of St. Ottilien. A short history of the Monasteries, General Chapters and Constitutions, Biographies of Its Superiors General. St. Ottilien, 1992.

B. Walter, Sustained by God's Faithfulness. The Missionary Benedictines of Tutzing, 2 vols. St. Ottilien, 1987-1992.

NOTES

1. There had been individual initiatives to recruit African candidates for the Abbey of Peramiho going back as far as 1926. Thus we read that "in 1948 several young men...expressed the wish to be accepted as candidates.... Archabbot Chrysostomus Schmid declined their request, however. He wanted local candidates to form their own congregation and instructed the Benedictine missionaries to undertake steps in this direction. Abbot-Bishop Eberhard Spieß (*Abbas nullius* from 1953-1969) eventually coordinated all these efforts. His main concern was to adapt the monastic life as far as possible to African conditions and to allow the candidates to integrate traditional African elements into their attempt to follow the Rule of St. Benedict. This would have been difficult in Peramiho as well as in Ndanda because the communities there consisted exclusively of European monks. Abbot Spieß therefore decided to start a formation house outside the abbey on a mission station. He chose a team of experienced missionary monks who, in 1956, began recruiting local vocations."

2. It was not easy for the monks to convince their neighbors that this region was fit for growing corn. The monks' success was first attributed to the power of special blessings and holy water. This belief lasted for something like five years, until the people began to plant corn themselves. This region has now become a granary for all of Tanzania.

3. Wood is generally needed as fuel and for construction. Until recent times, trees and bushes grew in insufficient quantities, and there was no perceived need for organized planting. Population growth, however, has made the consumption of wood a serious problem, as

there are no established patterns for planning for future generations. A monastic community, by its nature, thinks in longer periods of time and sets an example with the planting of trees for firewood and timber.

4. The comprehensive character of these cultural and spiritual centers can be seen e.g. from the famous ideal plan of a monastery conserved in the library of St. Gall with its internal and externals schools, the hostelries, the dispensary, its various gardens and stables, etc.

5. Of course, there is a big difference between the times of the Early Middle Ages and modern Colonialism, nevertheless there are common patterns and intentions.

6. The idea of setting up a monastery in the traditional sense collided with the idea of other missionaries to build up villages only for Christians where the newly baptized could be introduced into the Christian way of life.

7. From its inception the community of monks led, notwithstanding their extreme poverty, a strict monastic schedule in St. Benedict's, Pugu, following exactly the customs of the motherhouse. Cf. Renner II, p. 127.

8. In 1896 Ildefons Schober, abbot of Seckau and Superior General of St. Ottilien, and Maurus Hartmann, Prefect Apostolic of South Zanzibar, agreed to the so-called "Maria-Laach propositions" which set out a Benedictine way of evangelization and which corresponded both to the Benedictine principles and to the needs of the mission. Maria-Laach had been the place of their meeting.

9. To the Abbey of Peramiho belongs also the dependent priory of Uwemba, the monastic centers for all those Benedictine missions in the modern diocese of Njombe.

10. There had been long discussion about whether these monasteries should attempt to integrate local vocations or rather set up separate formation houses.

11. A delegation of the congregation headed by the archabbot expects to visit there in October, 1994.

12. The buildings of the monasteries of the monks and the sisters are still extant; the monastery of the monks serves now as military headquarters for the region; the sisters' convent is a dancing school.

13. Cf. Doppelfeld, and Sieber, p. 196.

14. Cf. Acts 2:47: "The Lord added to their number those who were being saved."

VIVERE IN CHRISTO*

Ghislain Lafont, OSB
(Abbaye La Pierre-qui-Vire,
St.-Leger, Vauban, France)

It is true that "the desert is a city." Yet, at the heart of this metaphor, which is also a reality, one can consider another which is just as real: "the monastery is a house." For a monk, to live in Christ (*vivere in Christo*) assumes the aspect, both immediate and spiritual, of living in a house. The blessedness of "those who dwell in the House of God" is truly his. And that is why I think that to speak of a monastery as a House of God and a house of monks is an authentic means of treating the theme *Vivere in Christo*.

So I shall take up this theme of the house and of the community that lives in it. In treating this subject, I prefer to keep to aspects which are common to all, very elementary, very concrete, and really down-to-earth. I shall use the same vocabulary as that used by the ancient Rules when treating of the monastic life: walls, places, food, drink, clothing, etc. This may seem to be a very lowly level of vocabulary, but in reality it is not, once we have grasped the profoundly sacramental character of all life in the Church. The way we lead our life in its most concrete aspects should be a reflection of the highest spiritual realities of faith unless, unfortunately, the reflection is distorted. The ancients were very well aware that those who take their surroundings, their body, their passions seriously are not far from the Kingdom of God—which is not necessarily true for those whose business is theology or spirituality!

The House of God

Let us do at least a little bit of theology to begin with, or rather let us renew our firm conviction of faith that if there is a house at all, it is the House of God. St. Benedict tells us this; it is an object of faith, a constantly renewed faith, and from time to time it must be re-evaluated. "House of God" means a house constructed by God in a definite spot to which he has set the boundaries; consequently, a house in which the monks are guests. This house is both the Body of Christ ("dwell in me") and the abode of the Spirit. "House of God" also means the house that God dwells in, and from this point of view, he is the host, and we could say that he is both the inside and the outside of this dwelling place. Thus we must constantly verify whether our concrete attitudes of faith and obedience correspond to this divine reality of the monastic house.

On the other hand, we must take a closer look at this twofold aspect of the House of God: the object of his attention, and whose center is his presence. This house, this monastery we live in, is not the only house that could be called House of God. Not only are there "many dwellings in the Father's house," not only is the universal Church the House of God, but the whole extent of the world and of the universe is also the House of God: "To God belong the earth and all it holds" (Ps. 24 [23]:1). Thus there must constantly be a concrete dialectic, whose terms should be defined and verified, between the inside (the particular location of the monastery) and the outside (the other Christian areas) and then all human areas. If, in order to build a house, there must be a roof which divides it from the infinite universe, and walls which divide it from the unbounded surface of the earth, there must also be doors and windows which bring together again what was divided. We must continually distinguish between living in a house and shutting ourselves up in it.

"House of God" is also a polyvalent symbol; it designates the concrete totality of the property and the buildings. But it also designates those who live there and who are "house" insofar as they are truly a community, not just borders or workers, but truly inhabitants.

Finally, each monk, for his part, is also a house of God, "formed" into a house of God just as Adam was formed of the primitive soil, and a host of God who invites Himself into His house. Anything that can be said about the "house of God" should be applicable, at one and the same time, to these three correlative realities: the place, the community, and the monk. Perhaps all the concrete work of the cenobitical monastic life consists in working towards the realization of an ever more perfect union of these three dimensions: spacio-temporal, communal, and personal.

The Spacio-Temporal Dimension

Architects of the past certainly had a more highly developed sense of symbolism than we have. When we look at a postcard of the overall view of some ancient monastery, we can say for certain at what time of the day the photo was taken. The church is oriented from west to east so that the altar would be illuminated by the rising sun; and the monastic buildings are spread out around the south wall of the church in such a way that, from morning until evening, the sun passes from one locality to the other, accompanying the monks as they carry out their daily duties. At the hour of Sext, for example, not only does the sun light up the whole nave of the church, but it enters into the eating areas, its warmth uniting with the heat from the kitchen hearth, and penetrates into the refectory, parallel to the church. These were things the monks didn't even notice because they were so evident. They were, however, full of meaning: was not Light the first work of the Creator, and "Sun of Justice" the name of the Risen One? If the reference to the sun and to light is correct, if the "body" of the monastery is well oriented, will the community not receive some of this light? Effectively, symbols have their function; they can be forgotten, as is, unfortunately, the case with us, and we should not consider it an insignificant loss. If the house is well oriented on the level of creation, Jesus' words (repeated seven times) in his discourse after the Last Supper, "Dwell in me so that you might bear much fruit," have already begun to be realized.

Whatever the case may be, we take the house and its placement as we find them. This is not just a matter of resignation, for it is by this that we grasp, at a primary and elementary level, the reality of a concrete tradition inextricably mixed with prophetical intuition and ephemeral interpretations. The walls left to us by our predecessors—the exterior ones to separate us from the outside, the interior ones to configure the inside—are a very meaningful language addressed to us which we must know how to interpret. They are the inscription in the earth and to a certain height, of a particular art of living the monastic values which were more or less important to them, or more profoundly, of their "religion," that is, of their way of perceiving the encounter with God through a certain use of material objects, sacred or profane. As monks of this monastery, we are their sons and their heirs by an unbroken chain. It is a good thing that we cannot demolish their walls, for thus perhaps we can continue to preserve their spirit.

However, it is a fact, a counterpart of the preceding, that every living monastery has, here or there, some kind of construction or renovation going on; the workmen are forever in the monastery for some job, big or small. Maybe this is some kind of a disease of monks, at least that is what some of them say. I would say that it is rather a sign of vitality. God is living and he never ceases to reveal himself anew. There are images of him, of his Christ, of the Spirit, and of the Church, which are being constantly renewed. Or at least there are perspectives, which even in their unfinished state, have influence on the aspect itself of the house of God. But man too is living and his relationship with the visible world, his fellowmen, or even with God, does not develop in exactly the same way today as it did yesterday. This constant evolution, which is not necessarily progressive, where we loose certain values to acquire others, where we forget and where we learn, is signified for those living in a house by renovations and transformations of the buildings. This was seen, more or less favorably, but in any case generally, in the remodeling of churches which followed the Council. It has a very profound significance, a new way of perceiving and of living the relationship between God and men (those in the community and those outside the community) and the relationship of men to God, less ritualistic perhaps, more sacramental and pneumatic. And the renovation of the church is most often accompanied by the transformation of the whole house, of which the concrete and immediate significance for monastic living is evident. Is there any monastery among those represented here, where the library has not been transformed, the kitchen modernized, provisions made for guest rooms, music rooms, even a television room, the cells and washrooms renovated? I am not saying that every monastery has done all the things I have just mentioned, but I think that they all have done at least something, and that the communities, when they took such and such a decision, were well aware that it was not neutral and without significance for the truth or the falsehood of the House of God, for the authenticity of the *Vivere in Christo*.

It is the abbot's place, it seems to me, to consider seriously both the permanency and the alteration of the walls and the roofs of his house without mentioning the gardens, the access roads, etc. The criteria used should not be based solely on the immediate need without taking into consideration faith or symbolism or beauty. One must take responsibility for the present as well as for the future, because what you undertake will not be entirely destroyed and, in a way, you define in advance a part of the spiritual heritage of those who come after you.

Thus, considered on the material level alone, of its walls and its actual layout, the House of God is already a symbol of the monastic life which is ours: the meeting place of a past, inscribed in the earth and in the forms, reminding us of a primitive generosity, but which also imposes on us real fetters; and of a future, when others will continue to live by the same Rule of Saint Benedict and the same traditions, in the buildings we shall have left them. Perhaps this is a reminder to live the present, in the concreteness of daily occupations, in a truly authentic way, that is, according to what we perceive as the truth of God, of man, and of nature, of which God is the confluence.

The Communal Dimension

In these buildings lives a community of people; they too are house of God, because they have been and are convoked by God. The first principle of unity in the community is that predestination by God of particular men or women to a certain monastic locality. Each one of us entered the monastery because he felt that here was his house and that these men would be—were already—his brothers. And this perception is without doubt even more vivid today than in the past, insofar as the young people

who come to us probably have, more than the preceding generations, a sense of the reality and of the importance of the community in the spiritual journey they wish to undertake. They
accept us without hesitation as brothers and expect us in turn to
treat them as such. They know, as if by instinct, that God does
not save men one by one, but some through others. Even if there
is in this view a certain measure of immaturity which needs to be
purified, the community, as a basic Christian reality, is for them
a kind of evidence; and we must let ourselves be converted to
this evangelic perception which, perhaps, we do not experience
to the same degree.

Effectively, we must begin with the community, this concrete
assembly of real people, living in this house and not another,
depository of, and responsible for a tradition in the sense that I
have just mentioned. Thus, it is beginning with the community
that we must continually pursue this work of discerning and
deciding, if the monks are to *live* (and here I distinguish between
"living" and "vegetating," that is, repeating without sufficient
reflection nor serious commitment, actions which do not concern
us very deeply).

The community should be the starting point for each and
every activity pursued in common; by this the community is
given form and motivation. I am not speaking here of the
elementary actions of prayer and cult, because they will be dealt
with in another conference, however, my perspective here is the
community, and I shall mention briefly what was perfectly
brought out in the preface to the *Thesaurus*, and that is that there
is an essential relationship between the community and its
prayer. This is simply a result of the perception of the Mystery of
the Church as developed by Vatican II, whereby the communion
of the local churches, united with and under the authority of
Rome and its bishop, was so well brought out. The prayer of the
Church is not necessarily accomplished by the fulfillment of a
particular program of prayers observed by all, wherever they
are, whatever be their vocation. It is realized by the spiritual
sacrifice of each community, united to all by the same Holy
Spirit, and in communion with the same Church. This variety in
unity is extremely difficult and demanding. I am not thinking
just of the enormous liturgical endeavor that it requires, which

we would often be tempted to abandon in favor of setting things down once and for all and never bringing up the subject again, but more especially of that constant demand that "our heart be in unison with our voice"—not only the personal heart of each monk, but the heart of the community. The spaces of freedom which are accorded to us for prayer and the verification of this prayer are of no use to us, unless there is among us the constant intention of *cor unum et anima una*, that is, of a truly spiritual freedom which unites us and permits us to find the true expression of our relationship, as a community, to the Lord. True liturgy builds up the community before God and in the Church, while reciprocally, our efforts to live truly as brothers constantly assures the quality of our liturgy.

Apart from the liturgy, we could use two classical Latin terms to describe the objectives of the community, *otium* and *negotium*, emphasizing, as has often been done, that the positive term, *otium*, designates the passive values of life, while the negative term implies the active output. For us monks it is particularly important, in the superactivity of today's world, to respect the primacy of the *otium*. This world expects, without being explicitly aware of it, the challenging testimony of communities where *otium* is of primary importance. Perhaps this is very often a subject of reflection and of discussion among abbots: Why is there so much overwork in our monasteries? How can we cast out the devil of excessive *negotium*.

Otium

As I said at the beginning of this conference, I shall keep this simple, which is also the preoccupation of the ancient Rules, because simplicity is essential to human symbolism: eating and drinking; sleeping and watching; dressing and, in our monastic perspective, remaining stable in one place. I believe that there is continuity between what could be called the stages of a symbol. Just as we eat our material food, so do we receive the word of God, so do we partake of the Body of Christ. A certain truth of *lectio divina*, for example, probably has something to do with the way we eat material food. I also believe that symbols have their own function, independent of our will; the way we live them creates in us human and spiritual habits which can be true, but which can also be false. So we must exercise a constant vigilance and discernment towards that which models our life, otherwise, we might be very different from what we think we are.

Food and drink. It seems to me that two temptations await us: that "fast food" where each one chooses his own from the self-service counter, whenever he wants it; and that of the family meal where—and rightly so—much care is taken in the quality of the food, in the atmosphere, and in the table conversation. In the world, meals are taken in one of these two manners, and even in monastic life both ways have their advantages, according to needs which are, for the most part, the same as those of other people: pressing work and the desire for a more convivial atmosphere. Perhaps these two types of meals could occasionally serve as an alternative to the usual community meal, in order to exploit the different possibilities of community living. I think it would be interesting to share experiments made in one or another monastery, the values discovered, the failures met with. We could also mention reading during the (let us call it the classical) meal. For example, in one or another monastery, more aware of the necessity of communication with those on the out-side, you sometimes have the impression that the reading in the refectory is the answer to the question which, according to the ancients, must never be asked: "How are things in the world?" In another monastery, the only universe ever mentioned is that of local history, of the good old days, of the priories no longer in existence, and of the saints of the past. That may seem like a small detail but, among other things, that is what gives a monastery a "style," what I called above a "religion." We need a religion; it is the abbot's place to decide which one it will be.

How could we leave this subject of food without mentioning briefly the question of fasting, which also has symbolic implica-tions? We used to faithfully observe the fasts of the Church which were quite strict; we even observed them when they were no longer prescribed. But gradually everything became more lax. I am aware that certain monks, of themselves, fast in solidarity, for example, with non-violence groups or to share in world hunger, but I am speaking here on the community level. How can we restore, without Pharisaism, without scruples, without overlooking the weak, the idea of a community that fasts, and for whom the instrument of good works *jejunium amare*, is actual?

Timetable. You certainly cannot construct a community with an open timetable, where there is no special time to retire or to get up. This is not a question of regulation in the military sense of the word, but of a profound understanding of the value of time, of the necessity of rhythm, of the benefits of certain repetitions which become ingrained in the community as a whole, and which free its attention for more important things. The *Vita in Christo* supposes a real *disciplina*, and perhaps this begins with the utilization of time. On the other hand, everything must not be so codified that there is never a free moment, thus risking the misunderstanding that time is a dimension which belongs to human creation. Without going into detail, I would like to say here that every monk knows well that the *disciplina* of monastic time should be qualitatively, if not quantitatively, marked by *otium* rather than by *negotium*; that the time spent in listening is more fundamental than that spent in speaking or in acting. Blessed are those communities, I think, whose timetable effectively respects this hierarchy of values.

The habit also is part of this style of *otium*. I may be mistaken, but I have the impression that, in the majority of cases, we are living a kind of division concerning the habit, to the detriment of our personal interior unity, that of the community and, perhaps also, of its testimony. Almost unanimously, we have kept unchanged the habit of our fathers, and we have not taken advantage of No. 7 of the decree *Perfectae Caritatis*. But is it really our habit? When we consider how often in one day we put it on and take it off again, you wonder if it has not become rather a ceremonial uniform—choir, refectory, even audiences with the Holy Father—while our real habit is civilian clothes. And in places where they keep it faithfully in its primitive form, is it as a symbol of integral observance or as a habit we live in, and by which we are recognized as men as well as monks? I have no answer to these questions, but perhaps a Congress is the place where they could be calmly discussed.

I suppose that, as abbots, you are aware from experience of the spiritual and monastic importance of such simple things as the timetable, the common table, a habit with both a human and Christian symbolism. You know from experience how important it is to strive for authenticity in these things, how difficult it is because of the resistance encountered, how beneficial or, on the contrary, how it hinders a certain quality of silence or ease in the practice of mutual charity. As for myself, I wonder if it is not by beginning with a real attention to chapters that we can make progress in two other important directions: the personal spiritual life of the monks, the *otium sanctum*, that taste for the things of God, which has its source partly in a sense for the things of man; and the *negotium*, activity, work.

Stability. One particular characteristic of the monastic community is that most of its objectives are pursued, as Saint Benedict says, in the enclosure of the monastery. In the world, a person has several spheres and several communities: his family, his profession, his parish, his sports club, etc. But they are different places which are not necessarily frequented by the same people; and each one must regulate this diversity so that conflicts are avoided. In the monastic life, we do not have the same situation: the *otium* and the *negotium* are practiced in the same place and by the same persons, and it is true for the divine cult as well as for the development of human culture. In the refectory we find ourselves with the same ones with whom we pray in the church; it is the same ones we meet again in the library, in the classroom, and the workplace, and it is still the same ones with whom we go for a walk or play tennis. In a word, the *inside* of a community is more intense than the *outside*. This constitutes a particular value and also some specific dangers.

First of all I would like to bring out its multiform values. From a theological point of view, it is clear that this concentration of goals in the same place and among the same persons emphasizes and realizes the intensity of the *Vivere in Christo*: to live in Christ is not just a spiritual attitude, a reflex of the soul; it is, gradually and through the grace of the Spirit, to lead back to obedience to Christ, human life in its entirety. Stability in a given place, fidelity to the same brothers, permits a community as a body and each of its members—and this is true of all the procedures which, day by day, contribute to the building up of society—our penetration of Christ and the availability required for

Christ's penetration of us. The limited character of space or number of persons, doubtlessly, permits an intensity which is not possible to the same degree anywhere else. There is relatively less loss of energy, less dispersed efforts, both human and spiritual, and, from a positive point of view, there is practically constant mutual aid. The themes of "microcosm" or of *ecclesiola* illustrate this: in the best instances, the community experiences, in faith of course, something of what Saint Paul means when he speaks of the Body of Christ as *pleroma*.

I also believe that stability in the community or, if you wish, stability *of* the community, is extremely favorable for the experience of salvation. On this subject I would like to point out two qualities which seem to me very characteristic of monastic and even religious life today. On the one hand, the work of returning to the sources and of the revision of Constitutions has certainly been positive for our communities. Even more, perhaps, than our immediately preceding generations, we have been led to reflect on what we are and to define what we would like to be. This reflection was undertaken in common in the monasteries; it led us to the rediscovery of a certain evangelic radicalism and a certain monastic authenticity, as well as to the expression of the desire, at least, to be faithful to these renewed perceptions. But, on the other hand, probably because of the fragility of human society to which we belong and the impact of technology, we are more conscious than before of our weaknesses—as persons, as communities; we all have our wounds, our short-comings, a real human insecurity. In this we are no different from other people of our time. The radiant, evangelic strength of the ideal coexists in us with an enormous fragility. But experience proves that the community is really a place of salvation; that is, it can be, if we come to consider it not so much as a "state of perfection" but rather as a humble school and, even more, as a place where we pass from our own perdition to God's salvation. The world we live in renders us and those who come to us, somewhat lost, somewhat as "misfits." The community should be able to help us experience healing and salvation. Here I would like to repeat what I have said or written on other occasions: The immense moral wisdom of the Fathers of monasticism should be alive once again in our monasteries, along with a rediscovery of the sacramental life as the living place of reconciliation and healing and a somewhat concrete understanding of human psychology and its workings.

Next, the values of monastic stability but also some specific dangers. On one hand, the monastic community trying *Vivere in Christo* by practicing stability, risks forgetting that it also belongs to larger spheres: that of the whole of monasticism, the Church, the world—this world we live in, whose face is changing so rapidly, whose form, recast by information, for example, and the constant shifting of demographics, will be so different tomorrow. So we must envision (and this might be a useful subject for discussion among abbots) the relation of stability in the community to the requirements which cannot be omitted in the formation of monks, for their health, for their communication with other Christian communities: how much non-stability is needed in order that stability be a symbol of life in Christ and not a chilly withdrawal of the community into itself.

On the other hand, we must consider who observes stability in the community and who talks about it; perhaps it is not the same ones. A large part of the monks observe it, those whom neither their formation, nor their talents, nor their work distinguishes enough to furnish an occasion for them to confront other ecclesiastical or human milieux. But does this stability "in fact" contribute to the development of their personality? or is it, on the contrary, an entombment, a barrier, a pity? More positively: under what conditions would it not be an entombment, a barrier, a pity? Those who talk about stability are certainly those, abbots or theologians for example, who observe it and esteem it, but who appreciate it even more because they have had the opportunity to meet others and understand better the value of monastic observance.

Negotium

It is not easy to talk about *negotium*, because the activity in monasteries is so diversified that it could not all be included in one general discourse. However, I believe that the subject should be addressed at this Congress. The Preparatory Commission thought of everything except that; I do not know why. Perhaps it is because when we speak of monastic life, we ascend spontaneously to the level of idealism, which in the admirable constructions of the eighteenth century was called the "noble storey"; and we never take into consideration, in spite of the insistence of the ancient Rules, life in the concrete: the common people of the chateau, the workshops. However, it is a fact. I shall limit myself to one remark: We belong to an old Order; our monasteries have, directly or through the houses by which they were founded, a long history. We have passed through centuries, and at all times we have been, somehow or other, a part of our age; then we have brought with us into the following age, some of the relics of the preceding one. From the point of view of work, it seems that we end up confronted with an impossible task: it is as if we believed it possible to respect all the values accumulated over the centuries. Are we not tempted to lead conjointly an outdated monastic life, centered on the works of asceticism, *lectio divina*, and await the Spirit, with just enough work to earn a living and give alms; a canonical life as in the Middle Ages, centered on a great display of the daily liturgy dominated by the solemnity of the conventual Mass; a life of study and/or of apostolate, as in the congregations founded after the Council of Trent, and all that with a new appreciation of work as an occasion for human development, and not just as penance or service? Perhaps we have to make choices in order to avoid, as much as possible, that disease of overwork which is too often ours; when it is not easy to take time to "live in Christ," because the activity in the community is too feverish and too dispersed.

Here I would like to add in parentheses that this question of the three lives that we are leading within the singular life that we should be leading is related to the difficult question (which I believe is very important) not only of the priesthood of monks, but of the relation between community life and the sacraments. As for myself, I hope that in the very near future a Congress would study this question. I understand that the theme of this Congress: "And you, who do you say that I am?" was chosen partly because certain abbots were worried about their monks' living faith in Jesus Christ. But in the monastic life everything is bound up together: if the concrete economy of the *sacramenta is* deficient, how can the *fides* be living and happy?

The Dimension of Hospitality

In what I have said so far, I have focused especially on the *inside* of the community, because that is the dimension which gives the first impression However, there is no inside without an outside, and for us monks, the outside comes to us more often than we go to it. In certain instances, however (parishes, missions), we, or several of us, go outside. Whatever the case may be, I would like to say a word about our hospitality—not to develop its possibilities and its demands, because a special conference will be devoted to that—but just from my point of view here: that of the monastic house. This hospitality takes many forms, the most important, I believe, are our guest houses, which are destined for spiritual hospitality, and our educational institutions, destined for the Christian and human formation of children, of young men, and of seminarians. For many reasons numerous people come to us. We give them our time, our strength, our knowledge, and our love. And we receive from them just about as much as we give them, if our heart is pure and poor—pure so that we do not keep anything back for ourselves; poor so that we might receive what is given.

In order that this multiform hospitality be in keeping with our cenobitic vocation, with the quality of our men living in a house of God, I think we should constantly verify that this mutual exchange between the inside and the outside is functioning satisfactorily. If people come to us in order to meditate or pray, if our relatives entrust their children to us for their education, bishops their seminarians for their formation, etc., it is because they have recognized our house as a house of prayer, and our community as a group of men seeking to love each other in truth, and who quite often succeed in this. Inversely, if we decide to have a guest house, to manage a school, a seminary, or a university, or any other service of this kind, it is not to do something useful alongside or outside of the monastic life, but because the tradition of our house or of our congregation has shown us a certain correspondence between these services of the Church and our vocation; and it is by these very services that our incorporation into the People of God is realized. Thus the unity of the community gathered under the same roof is the condition of the authenticity of its hospitality. I am not saying that nothing good can come out of a divided or overly dispersed community, but the fruit that our Lord expects from those who dwell in him runs the risk, in these conditions, of being more rare. On the contrary, the openness of the community to the People of God should be cordial, at the liturgy and elsewhere, because the church is our first house, and we have no reason to fear the entry of Christians under our roof and into our lives, if our interior cohesion in prayer and fraternal love is solid.

* * * * *

In closing this study, I am aware that I have rarely mentioned Jesus Christ explicitly, and from this point of view at least, if not from others, I have certainly disappointed you. My excuse is that the ancient Rules do not mention him very often either; they probably think that a way of life penetrated with a human truth that only the Gospel can give is, of itself, a revelation of Jesus Christ to those who live it loyally. I shall not, however, add any remarks at this point in order to make up for the inadequacy of which I am well aware, but I shall finish with a rather paradoxical conclusion which might provide food for thought.

Having said, with some conviction, all the preceding, I feel obliged to add this: the Bible is not very fond of the House; it prefers the Tent. It is more the book about displacement than about installation; about departures on the initiative of the divine Word than about stable possessions; of places passed through rather than any fixed territory, which is more the object of a promise than a gift—and with how many precautions and warnings it is given. The Son of God has nowhere to rest his head, and we do not have a permanent city here below. The Bible is more about wandering than about settling down; its perception of space is more longitudinal and dynamic than radial and fixed. And why is this so? Positively, because Christian existence is advancing towards an eschatology; it must at all times remain unattached and uninvolved, prepared for departure, even to go "there where you would not want to go." Negatively, because in the House or in the Temple we might set up other gods alongside the living God; not really chase God from his house, but impose companions on him, and get along well with all of them. We might also sacralize the traditions which, little by little, have become ingrained in the place, and no longer recognize God when he comes or goes. God becomes fixed in the image that the House has long ago made of him. Conservatism and casuistry get along well with idolatry in fact. We believe we are still living with God—and we are, in fact. But we are also living with many false gods: changeless customs, intrusive occupations, religious ideologies of all sorts; all, more or less consciously, baptized under the grand name of Tradition, unless, perhaps, falling into the opposite excess, we turn the house upside down in the name of Reformation.

So it is not easy to dwell in the House of the Lord and to adore in spirit and in truth. True stability is mobile, just like life, the definition of which scholasticism has passed down to us and which is not outdated: *motus ab intrinseco.* May Christ who calls us to "dwell in Him" obtain for us the grace to do it in that spirit of interior movement which will permit us to experience him as the Way, the Truth, and the Life.

NOTE

*This article is based on a conference given at the Congress of Benedictine Abbots held in Rome in September 1984. This explains the allusions to the abbatial office which appear here and there in the text, and the masculine thrust. The author, however, is using the word "monk" in its monastic sense to include both monks and nuns. Published in *Collectanea Cisterciensia* 47 (1985), 4-17. Translated by Sr. Anne-Marie Fitzgerald, OCSO, Abbaye N.-D. de l'Assomption, Rogersville, N.-B., Canada.

"TO PERSEVERE IN THE MONASTERY UNTO DEATH"*
(Stability in St. Benedict and Others)

Adalbert de Vogüé, OSB
*(Abbaye La Pierre-qui-Vire,
St.-Leger, Vauban, France)*

INTRODUCTION

1. An Initial Glance at the Rule of St. Benedict

a) The texts

The idea of stability appears in two areas of the Benedictine Rule: the spiritual section, comprising the Prologue and the first seven chapters, and the portion on recruitment.[1]

The Prologue ends by calling on its hearers to "persevere in the monastery unto death." A little further on, Benedict stigmatizes the instability of the gyrovagues and finishes off the "instruments of good works" with the declaration that, "The workshop where they are to put this into practice is the monastic cloister and stability in the community." While not quite as solemn as that conclusion, the recommendation found in the fourth degree of humility of "perseverance to the end, without giving up or going away" is no less clear and demanding.

Towards the end of the Rule a collection of practical precepts reaffirms the message of the spiritual treatises. The postulant is admitted only if he shows perseverance in his request for admission, and the first thing he is made to promise, either during his year of novitiate or at the end of it, is precisely that of "persevering" in a "stable" fashion throughout his life. These demands are imposed not only on the ordinary candidates but also on the "special cases"—priests and monks from elsewhere. All of them are required to "hold fast" and to "adhere," not just during the period of probation but even until the end of their lives.

b) The vocabulary

Despite the difference of context, one being spiritual and the other legislative, in describing this "stability" or "perseverance," both parts of the Rule employ the same vocabulary. Almost all of its various terms are derived from two etymological roots: first we have *perseuerare* and *perseuerantia*, and then *stare*, with its compounds *stabilis, stabilitas, stabilire*, to which *persistere* may be added. Only *firmare* is unrelated to these two groups and appears only once.

c) The ideal and its converse

The goal which is envisaged is obviously that of remaining for the whole of one's life in the monastery first entered, but this basic and constant theme differs somewhat according to whether it is opposed to one or the other forms of "instability," the gyro-vague character or apostasy. Most of the time it seems to be the second of these failures that Benedict has in mind, the abandoning of monastic life to return to the world. But at other times he attacks the behavior of certain individuals—the gyrovagues—who lay claim to being monks but spend their time passing through monasteries without settling down anywhere.

2. The Background: The Rule of the Master (RM)

a) The texts

This brief glance will be considerably more complete if we examine the literary background of the Rule of Benedict, beginning with its immediate source: the Rule of the Master. This deals with stability in the same two areas as Benedict's: the spiritual section, from the successive introductions up to the chapter on humility,[2] and the section on recruitment, which however begins a little earlier than in the other Rule, starting with the chapters on hospitality.[3]

b) The vocabulary

The terms the Master uses in speaking of stability are practically the same as those of Benedict, but with important differences in frequency of usage. He uses sixteen representatives of the group *perseuerare-perseuerantia*, whereas Benedict uses four. There are only three instances of the verb *stare* (the same number as used by Benedict) and six of *stabilitas* (seven by Benedict), while *stabilis* and *stabilire* do not appear at all; *persistere* (or *persistare*) appears four times (two by Benedict) and *sistere* once. But *firmare*, far from being unique as in the RB is found eleven times in RM, together with three *firmitas*, two *firmus*, one *firmiter*, one *perfirmare*.

The terms belonging to these three main roots—*perseuerare, stare*, and *firmare*—are in constant association in the Master's text. One perfect example of this multi-form and homogeneous vocabulary is provided by the first sentence of the chapter on profession: "When, following two months of reflection, the new brother chooses *stability*, decides to *persevere*, promises to adhere *firmly* to the Rule..."[4]

3. The Evolution in Vocabulary from the Master to Benedict

Without lingering over certain verbs which are used by the Master in exceptional cases—*fingere, habitare,*[5] and *remanere* (each used once), and *permanere* (used three times)—we should rather compare his use of the principal terms with that of Benedict, while remembering that the RM is three times longer than the RB. Given this overall ratio between the texts, the *perseuerare* group appears rather more frequently in the Master than in Benedict, and the *stare* group much more rarely. But the clearest difference is seen in the *firmare* group, whose eighteen members compare with only one representative in the other Rule.

Since Benedict comes after the Master and is dependent upon him, these facts show us the direction in which he readjusted his forerunner's terminology. He slightly lessened the usage of *perseuerare-perseuerantia*; he used *firmare* and allied terms hardly at all, while greatly favoring *stare-stabilitas* with the addition of *stabilis* and *stabilire*. To sum up, the seventeen cases of his usage of all these words expressing stability-perseverance are in correspondence with the Master's total of over fifty cases. The numerical importance of this vocabulary is the same for him as for his predecessor, but there is a change in the terms preferred.

I
AN ANTECEDENT: ST. CYPRIAN ON CHRISTIAN STABILITY

As Benedict shows such favor to *stare, stabilis* and *stabilitas*, it would be worth our while to consider the use made of these words before both him and the Master. There is one great Latin writer who claims our immediate attention because of his extensive and significant use of these very terms. We are speaking here of St. Cyprian, an author of prestige above all others—for Benedict as well as for the Master.

1. The Verb "Stare"

a) A military metaphor: "holding fast" and "falling"

Stare is one of the key words in Cyprian's works. In fact this verb expresses the attitude which was supremely appropriate in time of persecution: to "stand upright," "hold fast" without letting oneself be laid flat by the attacks of the devil, who tries to make one "fall" into apostasy. The *stantes* are those who stand up to intimidation and so are tormented, whereas the *lapsi* sacrifice to idols, denying their faith.[6] The image is that of the fighter who faces the enemy and holds on, as opposed to the one who crumbles and bites the dust. *Stare*, with this military meaning,[7] occurs at least thirty times in Cyprian's epistles, including letters addressed to him by various correspondents, and ten times or so in his treatises.

b) The metaphor's scriptural origin

It was not this great bishop-martyr and his friends who invented this language. The Apostles had already employed it: *state in fide*, said St. Paul to the Corinthian Christians,[8] echoed by—and the verb is not much different in Greek or in Latin—the *resistite fortes in fide* of St. Peter.[9]

The proof that these two New Testament exhortations are, partly at least, the source of Cyprian's and his friends' vocabulary, lies in the fact that *stare* is often accompanied in their writings by the adjective *fortis*,[10] the adverb *fortiter*,[11] and the prepositional phrase *in fide*.[12] The bishop of Carthage is inspired too by another Pauline text, the picture of the Christian who "holds on" in the battle against the devil, thanks to his being armed with the panoply of God.[13]

c) The application of "stare" to the struggle in time of peace

As in the New Testament, for Cyprian this image of the fighter who "stands" is applicable first and foremost to the great battle of martyrdom, of confession of the faith, or of simple fidelity in time of persecution.[14] But sometimes its meaning goes beyond this primary one of the battle for the faith. Besides the danger of apostasy, there are those of heresy, of schism, or of misconduct, ills which may affect, alas, confessing and faithful Christians as well as lapsi. Hence the extension of the military use of *stare* to the constant effort to resist the seductions of error and the pressures of bad Christians.[15] This peacetime struggle already makes one think of that of the monastic life.

d) Tendency to a spatial meaning

Moreover, would it not appear that the specifically military image of the warrior "holding fast" in the battle begins to take on another meaning at the time of Cyprian's writing his famous treatise *On Church Unity*? Twice in this treatise, *stare* appears in opposition less to the notion of "falling" than to that of "leaving."[16] Contrasted thus with *discedere* or *recedere*, the verb *stare* seems rather evocative of remaining in the Church and its peace, as opposed to "going away." Although still imprecise, this spatial connotation has particular interest for us, since, as we shall see, it is the one which characterizes *stare* as used by St. Benedict and the Master.

2. The Derivations "Stabilis" and "Stabilitas"

a) *Military and biblical echoes*

In completion of our inquiry into Cyprian's work, let us go on to consider *stabilis* and *stabilitas*. These words are used in the same warlike sense as *stare*, and with the same associations. Both in the singular and in the plural *stabilis* often follows *fortis*,[17] and it is accompanied once at least—as also *stabilitas*—by the prepositional phrase *in fide*.[18]

A fresh New Testament reference, and a very interesting one, is added to these expressions which, as we have seen, make allusion to the New Testament. Quoting Revelation, Cyprian calls on the confessors to be "faithful unto death," adding to the scriptural *fideles* the words *et stabiles et inexpugnabiles*,[19] as if these were quasi-synonymous terms. Thus we see "stability" associated with the impregnable constancy of the martyrs.

b) *A dynamic "stability"*

Stabilis and *stabilitas* occur several times together with the epithet *inconcussa*, giving the same idea of unwavering strength.[20] Even when used on their own, the adjective and noun are adequate to express that valor which nothing can overcome.[21] In Cyprian's writings these terms clearly mean a lot more than their equivalents in modern language. They are quite apart from the passive calm, immobility and static equilibrium evoked for us by the words "stable" and "stability." *Stabilis* and *stabilitas* mean active resistance, triumphant display of vigor, invincible persistence; in short, a display of total voluntary strength.

c) *Peacetime struggle and stability in prayer*

Stabilis and *stabilitas*, like the verb *stare* from which they are derived, are applied by Cyprian not only to the battle for the faith by confessors and martyrs, but also to the struggle of the faithful and of their pastors to persevere in Christian virtue, in obedience to God's commandments and the Church's discipline and communion.[22] Cyprian chooses a magnificent image to illustrate this "perseverance in faith and virtue," that of the arms of Moses raised in prayer throughout the battle against Amalek.

His two arms remained "stable" with the support of Aaron and Hur, and in his crucifixion-like stance in prayer, the perseverance of the man of God was also "stable."[23]

d) *Other connotations*

Stabilis has for Cyprian another less dynamic meaning, that of the feeling of security of one who is detached from the ephemeral world and resting in God.[24] Finally there should be noted in one of the above texts a contrasting motif found both in the Master and in Benedict: that of "departure." In stigmatizing the "unstable" schismatics, Cyprian contrasts them with the Church "which never leaves Christ."[25]

This *numquam ab eo omnino discedere* brings us back to the reflections provoked by certain uses of *stare*, in opposition to *discedere* or *recedere*, in the treatise *On Church Unity*. The noun *stabilitas* in the context of departure takes, like *stare* a spatial nuance which presages—from a distance—the use that the Master and Benedict would make of it.

3. From Cyprian to the Monastic Rules

Our two writers of Rules do not in fact give the same sense as Cyprian to the vocabulary of stability. Suggestive though the comparison with him is, it should not deceive us as to the distance separating the two Italian Rules from the African writings which antedate them by three centuries. For Cyprian, *stare* and its derivations describe a simple moral attitude: that of persevering in faith and virtue. The same words represent to the Master and Benedict a physical reality, which is certainly rich in spirituality, but above all consists of staying in a given place.

No doubt there is a real continuity between those two groups of terminology. Cyprian, on the one hand, gives them geographic significance—purely metaphorical, it's true—and often applies them to the Christian life's prolonged effort, considered in all its aspects and throughout its length, over and beyond the glorious but brief time of confession. On the other hand, the Master and Benedict have in mind a spontaneous, valiant and virtuous stability which, in its moral content, much resembles that of third-century Christians. Nevertheless the fact remains that the monk is bound to a new undertaking unknown to Christian spirituality at the time of the martyrs: to persevere *in the monastery* until death. This spatial element gives monastic stability true originality, when compared with that of Cyprian's contemporaries, while still being its genuine continuation.

It is not even possible, in the literary scheme of things, to state that one is derived from the other. Nothing proves that *stare, stabilis* and *stabilitas* occur in the Master's and Benedict's writings through Cyprian's influence. The latter's military metaphor is absent from their essentially concrete meaning and spatial object. Where the two vocabularies overlap it is not because the Rules are imitating Cyprian, but because the monk's situation is basically similar to that of the martyr, of the confessor and of the faithful Christian of every age. The use of the language of "stability" is the result of the necessity inherent in every Christian commitment to a persistent effort to "hold out" for a long time, even right to the end.[26]

II
BACK TO THE ORIGINS OF MONASTIC STABILITY

These comments inspire us to look for Benedict's and the Master's antecedents somewhere nearer to them, within the monastic movement to which they belong. This makes us think immediately of John Cassian

1. The Works of Cassian

This is not to say that Cassian is in the habit of using the words *stare, stabilis* and *stabilitas*.[27] Despite two characteristic uses of *instabilis* and *instabilitas*,[28] this is not his usual vocabulary. But the time of "perseverance" holds an important place in his writings where it appears in two guises: in Book IV of the *Institutes* Cassian extols cenobitic perseverance, consisting of spending one's whole life in the monastery one first entered; and in Book X of the work on the subject of *acedia*, he recommends the monk—the anchorite is particularly intended—to combat this vice by staying perseveringly in his cell. These two kinds of *perseuerantia* correspond to the two "stabilities" spoken of by the Master and Benedict, the one opposed to apostasy and the other to the "gyrovague" malady.

a) The cenobitic life and perseverance

The perseverance of Egyptian cenobites, which is long, endless and maintained into extreme old age, arouses Cassian's admiration. According to him it provides a contrast to the inconsistency of western cenobites, who cannot stand humble subjection to an abbot for very long. For it is not just a simple matter of staying in one place, but one of a genuinely spiritual perseverance, that of always keeping up one's original fervor and complete renunciation.[29] Scores of cenobites thus practice entire obedience to their superiors along with the complete dispossession which is a condition of it, right until death.

How then do the Egyptian monasteries obtain this astonishing result? Cassian thinks that such fidelity is due above all to the conditions imposed on entry and the strict requirements of the probation. The ten days' waiting period endured by the postulant, during which he is left at the gate with denials and insults showered on him, makes him understand at the outset that monastic life is a serious matter and has a price attached to it. After that the reception procedure, with all his money and even his clothes being taken away, initiates him in an effective and striking manner into the "poverty of Christ" which he must imitate all his life. Lastly, one year's service in the guest house of the monastery under the porter's orders teaches him obedience and humility, virtues which he will exercise in a still more demanding and spiritual manner after his entry into the community, when he will be under the charge of an elder or a "chief of ten."

Thus in Cassian's view, lifelong perseverance depends on perseverance at the beginning. By having a hard bout of patient effort imposed on him when he enters, the future monk's aptitude for holding out to the end in his new life can be ascertained. It is both a test of aptitude and a practical lesson; the rough welcome is a prelude to the rough existence and prepares one for it.

To persevere in one's request to be admitted and then to persevere until death, the double *perseuerantia* celebrated by Cassian
at the beginning of Book IV, is wonderfully illustrated by
Pinufius' story and discourse with which the book ends. Without
going into detail about these admirable pages, at least two new
features appearing in them are to be noted. First, there is the
quotation made by Pinufius from the Gospel: "He who endures
to the end will be saved."[30] The great abbot stresses that it is not
enough to make a beginning, as the person he is addressing is in
the process of doing. Christ's poverty and humility which he has
embraced on the day of his investiture he must in fact embrace
until death. While making an analogy between monastic commitment and Christian faith, this quotation of Christ's words
explains why the *usque ad finem* acts like a refrain in Book IV of
the *Institutes*,[31] before being taken up by the Master's and Benedict's Rules.

The other interesting fact to be gathered from Pinufius' discourse is that the commitment implied by taking the habit is
directed to perseverance in the monastic virtues, rather than to
stability in the spatial sense. Whenever Pinufius reminds the new
monk of what he has "professed," he is alluding to poverty and
humility,[32] or else to "perfection."[33] Of course it is understood
that poverty and humility are to be practiced on the spot, not
elsewhere, as perseverance in a given place is not the core of the
commitment, formally restated here. The spiritual aspect of perseverance is given more attention than its spatial dimension
receives.

b) Acedia and instability

By contrast, the "place" occupies the foreground in the pages
dedicated by Cassian to the struggle against *acedia*. One of the
most serious symptoms of this malady is in fact the *horror loci*,
distaste for one's cell and the temptation to leave it. Whence the
strong recommendation both in Book X of the *Institutes* and in
Conference XXIV,[34] to stay in one's cell come what may, and
therefore, to remain on the spot: *iugis cellae perseuerantia*,[35] *in loco
perseuerare*.[36]

Although usually applied to the anchorites' cells, this advice is also for the cenobites' monastery.[37] It is indispensable both for the former and the latter to remain where they are and busy themselves with work, for the principal cause of instability or acedia is idleness.

c) Colomba, Cassian's reader

Cassian gives such prominence to instability in his description of acedia that one of his most assiduous readers, St. Colomba, unhesitatingly substitutes *instabilitas* for *acedia* in a list of the eight evil spirits, making *stabilitas* the virtue opposed to this vice.[38] Without going quite as far as this pure and simple substitution, a short treatise attributed to Colomba *On the Eight Principal Vices* includes the *instabilitas acediae*, which is corrected by the practice of "stable meekness" and by "living in one place."[39]

This equating of acedia and instability soon after Benedict's time throws light on both his and the Master's Rules. When they speak on the subject of stability and instability, then we may at the outset think of the malady of *acedia* and the remedy for it, as they are so aptly analyzed by Cassian. Acedia, which Benedict mentions in connection with daily reading,[40] is more profoundly involved in the life-and-death matter of stability. It is good to reflect on it, remembering that, in the view of this whole tradition, the cure for acedia—and for instability—was to be found in work.

d) Keeping to one's cell come what may

Although linked mainly with acedia, the need for going out and for traveling is connected with other vices too. One to which Cassian gives only passing mention but which the Master views as the gyrovague's basic motive is the *gula*. On his tour of cells and monasteries, the unstable one has "an eye to nothing but this; viz., where or with what excuse he can presently provide for his next meal. For the mind of an idler cannot think of anything but food and the belly."[41]

Mother of vices, instability must therefore be avoided at any price. For Cassian, the precept of perseverance in one's cell is not merely the result of the reasons we have talked about. It turns up repeatedly in quite unexpected contexts, like a fundamental maxim to be stressed indefatigably. In the middle of the sublime discourse on spiritual progress, a speaker will stoop to the advice of never leaving one's cell; each exit is an irreparable loss.[42] Further on, during a dissertation on demons, he quotes the command the ancients gave to monks afflicted with spiritual languor: "Stay in your cells. There you may eat, drink and sleep as much as you like provided that you stay there without shifting."[43]

2. The Apothegms

Sedete in cellulis vestris. This instruction cited by Cassian is to be found, in the singular, in more than one apothegm.[44] *Libellus* VII of the systematic collection translated into Latin by Pelagius and John—among Benedict's favorite reading matter—reproduces it four times,[45] without counting numerous other similar exhortations.[46] Of all the forms that the monk's "patience and strength"—which are the subject of the *Libellus*—have to take, hardly any is more highly recommended.

From among all these appeals to stability, let us take at any rate two, which Paschasius of Dumio, another translator, unites in a single apothegm.[47] According to this, the cenobite ought no more to leave his monastery than a bird its clutch of eggs—there is an identical risk of cooling down and infertility—or a tree, the ground where its roots are; if transplanted several times,[48] it will never bear fruit.

3. The Tradition of Lerins

We must now turn from the apothegms, where Cassian led us, to the literature which is, properly speaking, cenobitic and Latin, and in it look for the rudiments of a doctrine of stability, both pre- and post-Benedict.

a) The Rule of the Four Fathers

At the start of the tradition of Lerins, c. 410, the Rule of the Four Fathers makes no mention of a commitment to perseverance when dealing with the admission of postulants. As Cassian reports for Egypt, the candidate being left outside the door for a week certainly has to "knock perseveringly,"[49] but the directives about training given to the superior speak only of obedience, humility and dispossession, without breathing a word about the time or place where these virtues are to be displayed.

The question of stability does not emerge until the matter of monks from elsewhere comes up. The Father, namely Macarius, whose turn it is to speak in this appendix, shows such people great severity. Quoting from St. Paul, he prohibits not only the receiving of, but even the seeing of a brother from another monastery, who has come without his superior's consent, since he has "denied his original faith" and is "worse than an unbeliever."[50]

The conditions of admission subsequently laid down by Macarius tally with these clear allusions to a commitment of perseverance: the monk has to have been recommended by his former superior, and has to take the lowest place, as a token that his monastic age, linked with his membership in his original community, is annulled by his having left it; he is required to begin his life all over again, in complete dispossession and humble subordination.[51] Nothing is omitted that would cause him to feel that his life has been shattered by the departure from his monastery.

b) The Second Rule of the Fathers

In 427, the Second Rule of the Fathers, which is also the Second Rule of Lerins, specifies on two occasions that no brother may leave the precincts, whether to go where he wants without his superior's permission,[52] or to escape punishment from his superior.[53] Although the matter here has to do with enclosure rather than with stability, nevertheless these regulations are not irrelevant to our subject, for the two questions are inseparable, as we saw with Cassian. To remain at one's post is the common principle which is breached by occasional escapades as well as by definitive flight, and by illicit excursions, as by apostasy. The transition from one to the other of these misdemeanors is often imperceptible and it is difficult to make a distinction, with the texts being applicable to either.

c) The Sermons of Faustus of Riez

Following the Second Rule of the Fathers of Lerins, tradition was personified by the great abbot, Faustus of Riez, for some twenty-five years. In his homilies to the monks he lays exceptional stress on the value of "the place," but also on its insufficiency. No other writer, whether before or after Benedict, has given such prominence to the notion of stability.

Homily XXXVIII of "Eusebius Gallican" (Faustus' pen name) shows, first of all, the importance of the place where God has called us, enlightened us, and given us refuge against the world's tempest. One cannot leave it without being really uprooted. One can say that all is not lost, that one still has the monastic habit and will live in the world as a monk. But what a sad return it is, like a ship returning in a sorry state to port, bereft of its cargo.[54] One will repent of it; it serves no purpose when one carries along the malady that causes one to leave. In reality one is inflicting the worst of punishments upon oneself.[55] Instead of being better off elsewhere, one will regret having left the fold, broken with one's brethren and left the premises without the kiss of peace.[56]

In the next Homily, Faustus qualifies his praise of the "place"—this being the island and monastery of Lerins— emphasizing the inadequacy of a presence spiritual as well as physical. Living in this desert place avails nothing if worldly passions are borne within oneself. In vain does one enjoy the tranquillity of the place with one's body if one's heart remains troubled.[57]

Similar qualifications appear at the beginning of Homily XL: no security results from living among God's servants or on the island—even if one does so for fifty years together.[58] However, here Faustus' reflections turn to the exalting of stability: "In order to make our earthly race pleasing to God, we must practice stability and perseverance, persisting until the end in the place to which we shall finish.... The success of all our efforts will be decided at the last moment."[59] Having dispelled the illusions of anyone thinking of being able to leave without harm after four or five years, the Abbot of Lerins concludes: "Let us therefore be stable, as far as we can manage, in this tranquil harbor. However negligent and lukewarm one may be, one will not have run in vain when, through perseverance, one attains the palm of those who have gone on right to the end."[60]

And so this meditation on the monk's "place" ends with an unreserved commendation of stability. What Cassian and the apothegms said of perseverance in one's cell, Faustus repeats on the subject of the monastery. Just as the anchorite, even though without much zeal, is saved only through the fact of staying within his four walls, so also the cenobite, even if negligent, will not fail in his life if he perseveres. Stability is the sheet anchor for them both.

d) The Rule of Macarius

One of Faustus' successors, Abbot Porcaire, is probably the author of "Macarius' Rule," in which the battle for stability is continued. The monk who cannot bear being reprimanded and threatens to leave is chastised with rods. He who goes off slamming the door behind him will receive nothing but secular clothing which, it is specified, will be "altogether ridiculous."[61] In the rough way befitting this end of the fifth century, with Provence having fallen into the hands of the barbarians, everything is done to prevent departure, make it odious, or limit the damage caused by it.

e) The Third Rule of the Fathers

Forty years or so later, the series of minor statutes produced by Lerins is brought to an end with the Third Rule of the Fathers, emanating most probably from the Council of Clermont (535). Misdemeanors committed by monks going out have a considerable place among those penalized by the bishops.[62] But the most important fact is that the document's authors, like the Four Fathers, legislate finally on monks changing from one monastery to another. To be received elsewhere, not only has the monk to present his abbot's permission; he has moreover to be motivated by seeking a "stricter rule," which he will henceforth be forbidden to abandon.[63]

f) Other episcopal ordinances

This last article from the Third Rule is all the more interesting in that it relies upon the twenty-seventh canon of the Council of Agde (506), which followed the way opened by the sixth canon of the Council of Vannes (461-491). Remembering that the Bishop-monk Ferreol of Uzes came back to this question,[64] it seems that monastic stability was a subject of ceaseless preoccupation to the Gallic episcopate of these two centuries. For both Ferreol and the Council of Vannes, this problem is closely in keeping with that of the stability of ecclesiastics. The unstable and wandering, whether monks or ecclesiastics, are a blot on the Christianity of this period. And not only in Gaul. The bishop of Aquileia, like the bishop of Arles, is informed by Pope Leo of vagabond ecclesiastics, taking their "instability" from one Church to another.[65] In reading his complaints, one has the feeling of listening already to the satire on the gyrovagues, which makes up the Master's first chapter.

III
THE MASTER, BENEDICT AND OTHERS

This glance at monastic literature prior to the Master and Benedict's epoch will enable us to put into perspective their remarks about stability.

1. The Master's Opening Definition, and Further References

Without going at length into their criticism of gyrovagues— brief with Benedict, interminable with the Master—we must consider primarily the first passage in which perseverance is spoken of, the solemn presentation of the monastery-school which ends their respective introductions (thema or prologue): "Therefore we must set up a school of the Lord's service, to the end that, never abandoning this master and persevering in the monastery with his teaching until death, we may deserve to share in Christ's passion through patience, so that the Lord make us also co-heirs in his kingdom. Amen."⁶⁶

This admirable conclusion not only contains the definition of the monastery as a *schola*,⁶⁷ but also that of monastic life as perseverance in this school of the Lord. To grasp its complete significance it has to be put side by side with several of the similar phrases to be found in the Master's spiritual section and in his practical legislation.

a) The Master's "ars sancta"

This is not, in fact, the only time that the Master makes "perseverance" the last word in a spiritual exposition. The list of virtues he sets down in Chapter IV ends with *perseuerentia usque in finem*;⁶⁸ nor is it in vain to observe that the list of vices which follows ends likewise with *vagatio*, i.e., instability.⁶⁹

Somewhat later, the whole section on the *ars sancta* leads up to the presentation of the workshop where this spiritual "trade" is exercised: "The workshop is the monastery. There it is that the work of divine art is achieved, through constant effort and by means of perseverance."⁷⁰ In this concluding sentence the Master repeats the final statement of his *Thema* almost identically. School and workshop, the monastery is the unique, irreplaceable site of the spiritual labor which saves the monk. For all work, the first and indispensable condition is to persevere in it.

b) The fourth degree of humility

As for "patience" and "sharing in Christ's sufferings," which form part of this perseverance, these are the subject of a splendid portion in the middle of the treatise on humility. At the fourth rung on his "ladder up to heaven,"⁷¹ which is only exceeded in size by the first rung, the Master goes at great length into that "patience" which makes one keep on "without wearying or giving up."⁷²

Non discedat: Here one recognizes the *nunquam discedentes* from the end of the *Thema*. But the two passages agree above all in making the aspect of the painful struggle of this faithfulness stand out. Without it being a matter explicitly of "sharing in

Christ's suffering," the fourth degree of humility speaks in similar fashion of trials "overcome for the sake of the one who loved us."[73] In two parallel passages, before and after the chapter on humility, the Master goes as far as comparing the obedient monk's patience with the passion endured by the martyrs.[74] Thus one returns to the theme, dear to Cyprian, of the heroic perseverance of those persecuted; monastic stability is equated with that of martyrdom.

Of all the scriptural quotations adhering to this fourth degree, we must cite at least that from the Gospel: "He who endures to the end will be saved."[75] This statement of Christ which is cited first of all reminds us particularly of the conclusion of the *Thema*: "to the end" being equivalent to "unto death." Besides this, it recalls Pinufius' discourse related by Cassian.[76] But whereas the latter intended of it perseverance in the cenobitic virtues of poverty and humility, the Master connects it more precisely with stability of place; "to persevere until the end" is "not to go away."

c) Scriptural references at the end of the "Thema"

The abundant and explicit scriptural illustrations of this degree are in contrast with the discreet allusions to which the Master restricted himself in the conclusion of the *Thema*: "to persevere *usque ad mortem*" resembles the words of Revelation, "Be faithful until death," no less than the description of Christ's obedience in the Letter to the Philippians.[77] As for *perseuerare in eius doctrina*, there one perceives an echo, whether deliberate or not, of the "persevering devotion to the Apostles' teaching" which characterized the Christians of Jerusalem,[78] and even more of the "abiding in the doctrine of Christ" which is mentioned in a passage—not well known, it is true—of the Johannine letters.[79]

d) The legislative section of the Rule of the Master

Light is thrown on the riches of sense in this conclusion not only when attention is paid to its biblical reference and to the reminders of it which occur in the spiritual part of the Rule. It should be compared also with at least three passages where the Master says the same thing in the practical section of his book.

Thus one perceives that this is not just a spiritual formula expressing an ideal program; it is a down-to-earth requirement, the working of which is enforced with the maximum of method and realism.

On the matter of guests, to begin with, the Master takes the case of traveling monks—we are not referring to "gyrovagues"—who settle in after staying in the guest house for a while. Then, following the two months of reflection given to every postulant, "they will give themselves to the monastery to persevere there until death."[80] What was presented in the conclusion of the *Thema* as a desirable result and a vocation here becomes the object of a veritable commitment.

In a latter chapter where the Master deals with secular candidates, they too are warned that they will not be able to leave without doing themselves great harm, spiritually as well as temporally. The "guarantee of stability" that they have had to subscribe to holds that "if ever they wish to leave the monastery, it will be without taking any of their possessions and without pardon for their sins that they leave God."[81] This sentence, employing the verb *discedere* twice, turns the exhortation at the end of the *Thema* "never (to) leave the teaching of Christ" into an explicit threat.

Finally, the economic aspect of these precautions is subjected to a searching light in one of the last pages of the section on recruitment. Being unable to take away anything of the goods they have brought, "by these means the disciples will be retained in God's school, and, for want of something better, their belongings will make them stay in the monastery."[82] These somewhat cynical considerations are condensed in the form of a maxim: "Perseverance gains footwear and clothing, departure renders the things due to the monastery, and then (he) goes off, if he wishes."[83] Staying in the monastery, persevering there or going away, these terms from the conclusion of the *Thema* all recur here in the rules that can scarcely be more realistic, with the beautiful ideal stated before taking on a rather unpleasant air.

2. From the Master to St. Benedict

Such is the genius of the Master, at once capable of the highest spirituality and of the most down-to-earth attitudes. We have now to compare his thought with that of Benedict. This is not easy, for the latter is much less abundant and less explicit.

a) The spiritual part of the Rule

The conclusion of the *Thema* and the fourth degree of humility are copied by Benedict without any notable changes.[84] In contrast, the "persevering until the end" and its opposite, *vagatio*, do not appear in the Benedictine Rule, the lists of virtues and the vices not having been incorporated into it.

As for the monastery-workshop, this we do find in Benedict but along with some new terms, whose significance is not obvious: a more forceful expression: *claustra monasterii*[85] corresponds to the Master's simple *monasterium*; moreover *perseuerando* is replaced by *stabilitas in congregatione*. We have already noted Benedict's preference for the vocabulary of "stability." By adding "in the community," is he not merely concerned with the balance of his sentence? "The community" is indeed the "monastery" taken in its human, living aspect; yet does the writer intend anything by this term other than a convenient synonym and a way of avoiding repetition?

b) Legislation

Things become clearer when one comes to the legislation. Here there emerges a notable difference between the two Rules. In that of the Master, no explicit promise of perseverance was contained in the ceremony of profession. No doubt the matter was quite clear because of everything said previously and everything that followed, that the new brother was committing himself to staying indefinitely. But in the chapter on profession, stability was mentioned only in the preliminaries to the rite and its conclusion.[86] In the course of the ceremony, the professed monk promised simply to "serve God according to the Rule in the monastery."[87] The final words *in monasterio tuo* defined the place of divine service without specifying its duration.[88] Only the written statement which the professed laid on the altar, in certain cases, formally considered the possibility of a departure, and condemned this.[89]

This is not so for Benedict. Stability here is not only promised as a preliminary; it is also solemnly professed in the liturgical rite. At any rate one understands this from the rubric *promittat de stabilitasua et conversatione morum suorum et obedientiam* which is Benedict's description of the promise made in the oratory before everyone, and in the presence of God and of his saints.[90] This threefold oral promise, which is consigned in writing—the *petitio*—and placed by the professed on the altar, has *stabilitas* as the first article. Thus the commitment to stability is made public and explicit. This is no longer just a clause which is assumed, but a formal, even primary, article of the pact established between the professed and God.

3. Around Benedict and the Master

The position given to the promise of stability in our two Rules should be compared with certain measures taken in Gaul at this time, and in Spain in the succeeding century.

a) Legislation of Caesarius

The two Rules by Caesarius of Arles reveal another progression in this field. According to the Rule of Virgins, any sister who entered "would never again leave the monastery until her death."[91] This solemn warning at the beginning of the Rule refers less to stability than to enclosure, as shown by what follows: Caesarius states here that the sister cannot "even go into the basilica" adjoining the monastery. Thus it is not a direct matter of perseverance, but one of strict separation from the world, a concern which perpetually haunted the founder-bishop. He insists on every page that superiors and portresses should be watchful of this point, even designating certain doors condemned by him, whose re-opening is to be forever forbidden.[92] As for the "profession" of new sisters, this has for its object the observance of the Rule,[93] with no explicit mention of stability.

The monks' Rule, in contrast, demands at the outset perseverance until death.[94] Caesarius here repeats the beginning of the Rule for Virgins and modifies it; instead of *de monasterio non egrediatur*, he writes *ibi perseueret*, specifying that this perseverance in perpetuity is a "condition of admission" placed before every candidate.

So one goes from the enclosure imposed on the nuns to the stability demanded of the monks. This is nothing but a nuance, as enclosure obviously implies stability. But in Arles and Italy alike stability or perseverance—one and the same thing—is the subject of an altogether formal obligation, after having been demanded in a less explicit manner. Although the reasons may be different to some extent,[95] the evolution in Caesarius' legislation is analogous with that which we have noted in comparing the Rules of the Master and Benedict.[96]

b) The Spanish Rules

As with Caesarius' Rule of Monks, the Spanish Rules of the seventh century insist upon a commitment to stability from the time of entry. Indeed they go so far as making it written. In laying down this edict, Isidore of Seville suggests a suitable comparison: "Just as, in the world, those admitted to military service do not enter the legion before being put on the roll, even so in the spiritual camps, those about to receive the insignia of the heavenly militia do not enter the army of Christ's servants without first having made a written or oral commitment."[97]

These last two words not withstanding, it was a written deed that Isidore had prescribed a few lines earlier,[98] and which his reference to military usage suggests.[99] This parallel ties the monk to his monastery as the legionary to his legion. While there is nothing original in the comparison between a monk and a soldier, the one between monastic profession and the enrolling of a legionary is new, as far as we know. One would like to know just how far it really influenced the Isidorian edict.[100]

Fructuosus of Braga, in turn, puts this provision into his Rule: the new arrival must deliver to the abbot a *pactum*, containing a written promise to observe the Rule.[101] But perhaps here it is less a commitment to stability than one to enclosure: the brother promises only not to roam about far from the monastery to which he has "bound" himself. Yet the two questions are so interconnected—let us take note of this once more—that Fructuosus may well have both in mind. In any case, his legislation *pactum* makes any illicit departure to "live" elsewhere condemnable in advance, in terms which make one think of real offenses of instability.[102]

c) Two pages from Gregory the Great

Many other points inspired by Fructuosus concerning stability could be taken from the *Regula Communis*.[103] However, we would like to finish our inquiry by bringing it closer to Benedict in both time and space, and also by raising it from the judicial to the spiritual level. Our last indications come from Pope Gregory, the saint's biographer.

The first is found in the *Dialogues*. A recluse who had chained himself with an iron chain to the wall of his cavern was told by Benedict: "If you are God's servant, be not detained by an iron chain but by the chain of Christ."[104] This praise of the chains of love gives value to any bond of monastic stability and enclosure, quite apart from the borderline in the case of the one chained voluntarily.

The other interesting text is in the *Commentary on Kings*. Gregory says a lot about monastic life in this work of his closing years. Although not giving stability as much prominence as obedience, he exalts it nevertheless in one short but notable passage. The subject is the return of the Ark of the Covenant to Israel by the Philistines. The cart stopped when it reached the field of Joshua at Bethshemeth. *Et stetit ibi.*[105] Gregory, for whom the people of Bethshemeth represent contemplatives, sees a symbol of their perseverance in this halting of the Ark among them. His commentary:

> ...while the life of withdrawal from the world results in the joyful spectacle presented to it,[106] yet it also has to maintain a great effort in the valiant combat which has to be fought. For after the victory, divine rewards are granted to us but then we have to keep them by fighting valiantly. Hence the relevance of the words about the cart coming into the field of

Jesus (Joshua): "It stopped there." "To hold still or stand (*stare*)": the verb implies the vigilance of the combatant and not the tranquillity of peace. So the cart "stood in the field," for if our mind already abides in the vision and love of the charms of that verdant celestial country, it is not without incessant care and watchfulness that it conserves what pleases and enchants its eyes.[107]

Thus, in the view of our commentator, imaginative and expert in monastic life, the Ark's "stand" represents the strenuous effort monks have to exert continually in order to "stand" in their paradise. Making a play on the double sense of the verb *stare*, Gregory associates military courage with monastic stability. This is a return to Cyprian and his martial vocabulary. While the martyr of Carthage applied it to the Christian's fight for faith, the *stare* of the soldier holding firm on the battlefield recalls the monk's struggle for perseverance. Hence the effort called for by the latter is fully brought to light. It is less a case of immobility in one spot than of grit in battle. Monastic "stability" is not inertia, but valor.[108]

CONCLUSION

Has this brief review of a few landmarks in tradition thrown light on the meaning of the monastic stability extolled by Benedict? Perhaps, at any rate, it has conveyed the richness of this concept and its history.

1. A Short History of Stability

Its sources are to be found in certain New Testament texts: "He who endures to the end...";[109] "Stand firm in your faith";[110] "Resist him, firm in your faith";[111] "Be faithful unto death."[112] Not only do these inspired sayings provide the notion of endless persistence and an unfailing constancy, they also give the two verbal roots by which this mysticism of fidelity is expressed—in Latin, at least—*perseuerare* and *stare*.[113] Yet it is still simply a matter of moral perseverance and stability, in adherence to the faith

and the practice of the Christian life. In paleo-Christian literature, the same idea returns, for instance, to a Cyprian, who from
these apostolic texts, evolves magnificently the idea of the bat-
tling Christian: "Holding firm" in the confession of the faith in
times of persecution, as well as in the Church's discipline in time
of peace. It is rare for a connotation of place—"staying on the
spot"—to tinge these metaphorical ways of using *stare* and its
derivatives.

Stability-perseverance acquires a new significance with
monasticism. While remaining an essentially spiritual concept,
it finds tangible expression in permanence in one place. The
ancient intention of heroic fidelity to the Lord is carried over to
the anchorite's cell and the cenobite's monastery. When weary of
his cell, the hermit states: "I keep to these four walls because of
Christ."[114] In the eyes of the Master and Benedict, to "persevere
in the monastery" is to "persevere in his teaching"—that of
Christ.

Thus a geographical factor is added to the one of duration.
The monk's persevering stability, being both spatial and temporal, is akin to reclusion. We have frequently noted this connection between stability and enclosure.

2. The Question of Pilgrimage

Must pilgrimage be added to the breaches of the principle
of stability, some more serious than others, represented by
apostasy, change of monastery, escape from the cloister and
gyrovagy? Let us be clear; by pilgrimage we do not refer to the
vast phenomenon of *peregrinatio*, leaving one's country for a
religious motive, which has been studied recently by others,[115]
but to a more limited case, the journey *ad loca sancta*, in order to
visit a holy person, or a holy place and be edified by this experience. Recognized generally as praiseworthy for ordinary believers, is this devotional practice also suitable for monks?

We shall not dispose of very much evidence to enable us to
answer this question. The ancients do not seem to have ever
asked it. Only incidentally do we hear through Cassian about
Egyptian cenobites on pilgrimage to the holy places in Palestine.[116] On the other hand, Cassian himself undertook a pilgrim-

age to Egypt with his friend Germanus, while both were cenobites at Bethlehem. Having left with their elder's permission, but on condition that they would shortly return, the two young monks broke their promise after a battle of conscience as related in Conference XVII. So for the great Egyptian monks the pilgrimage was transformed into a stay of indeterminate length. The superiority of anchoritism over the cenobium and of monastic Egypt over Palestine appeared to legitimize this patent infraction of stability.

That the ancient monks, even cenobites, did go on pilgrimage can be proved by a multitude of similar examples.[117] They sometimes went outside for simple devotional reasons, to satisfy the spiritual desire to visit such and such a place, quite apart from the business journeys which are often mentioned in the texts. The fact that neither the Master nor Benedict—nor any other writer of a Rule—refers to such journeys merely shows that, in contrast to business trips, they are regarded as exceptional journeys which are often mentioned. Pilgrimages must have been rare events, without having been totally forbidden. One is aware of the very restrictive attitude taken by our two Rules on the subject of going out.[118] It could only be in case of "necessity." The estimating of necessity, while rather lenient in the matter of practical needs, was probably much stricter when it came to spiritual impulse.

3. The Good Stability

In effect—and this is the note we would like to end on—the whole of the tradition to which our two Rules belong attaches the highest importance to stability of location, taken as far as the most minute rules of enclosure. Egyptian monasticism was fundamentally sedentary,[119] in contrast to other milieus where peregrination was a possibility,[120] and western monks essentially owe to it a cult of stability which they had developed in an original way. Doubtless, the ecclesiastical concern for order united itself to monastic Egypt's peasant instincts, and monks, like ecclesiastics, had to belong to a place and abide in it. But such canonical considerations are much less important here than the profound spiritual motives arising out of Egyptian experience.

Cassian, who was its spokesman, brought out the worth of the cell as a symbol and message of recollection. There, and there alone, could the soul be attentive to itself as well as to God.[121] As for the monastery, we will know with what esteem the Master and Benedict, following Cassian, held "perseverance" within its walls.[122] For to them the monastery is seen as the school of Christ, practically exclusive in spreading his teaching, with its masters the only ones qualified to make known the Lord's will and put it into practice.

This very exalted idea of the monastery, of the life which is led there and the work accomplished there, alone serves to explain the demands of perpetual stability. If the monk has to persevere in his cloister until death, it is because there, and only there, so one thinks, something great and irreplaceable takes place. The law of stability presupposes a high evaluation of the observances practiced in enclosure: that of continued prayer shown in the offices and continued through work and reading; obedience, silence, and humility; the fraternal life of service and charity; asceticism in food and sleep; and so on. Not for nothing is *stabilitas*, in the rubric of professions, followed by *conversatio morum* and *obedientia*. For it is the infinitely precious whole formed by the monastic virtues and observances, as found in these two terms, which constitutes the motive of the primary demand for unfailing perseverance.

NOTES

*First published in French in *Collectanea Cisterciensia* 43 (1981) 337-365. This English translation was read at the Fourth Seminar on Hindu and Christian Spirituality (Asizvanam, 1982).

1. Rule of St. Benedict (RB), 58-61.

2. Rule of the Master (RM), Prologue 10.

3. *Ibid.*, 79-91. With the addition of the chapter on the return of the prodigal (RM 64). For the references in detail, see the concordance on *La Règle du Maître*, vol. III, Paris, 1965 (*Sources Chrétiennes* 107); *La Règle de Saint Benoît*, vol. II, Paris, 1972 (*Sources Chrétiennes* 182), pp. 679-860.

4. RM 89.1, *Cum...ab eis magis stabilitas eligatur, et perseuerantia, repromissa lectae firmitate, ab eis placeat adinpleri...*

5. RM 87.57. This verb is used twice, apart from this, in speaking of temporary stays (RM 87.3 and 64), which are also denoted by the verb *remorari* (RM 79.29 and 33; 87.60).

6. Cyprian, *Ep.* 10.4,4; 33.1, 2; 55.51. The same language is used in letters of the Roman clergy (*Ep.* 30.5.3; 30.6.2; 36.3.3) and confessors (*Ep.* 31.6.2). *Qui statis* (43.7.1) and *steterunt* (60.2.5) are also found, together with the infinitive *stare* in contrast to *iacere...prostrati* (25.1.1), *deicere...prostratos* (61.3.2), *uicti et prostrati* (65.1.2), and *deficere* (67.8.2), or alone (56.3.1). In this last case and in two others (25.1.1; 60.2.5) the subject is *lapsi* who arise and continue the fight. Here we quote the numbering given in *Saint Cyprian, Correspondence*, vols. I-II, publ. Bayard, Paris, 1925, which follows that of Hartel (Vienna, 1868; LSEL 3) and differ from that of Migne, PL 4.

7. The military metaphor is particularly clear in *Ep.* 12.2.2 (*stantes et...fortiter dimicantes Christi castra non dereliquerunt*); 28.2.1 (*stare firmo gradu*); 56.2.1 (*stetisse in acie*); 56.3.1 (*stare fortiter et pugnare*); 60.2.5 (*steterunt...ad praelium fortiores*); 65.1.1 (*in praelio fortiter stare*); 67.8.2 (*stetisse et certasse*).

8. 1 Cor. 16:13.

9. 1 Pet. 5:9.

10. *Ep.* 8.3.4 (Roman clergy); 10.2.2; 60.2.5.

11. *Ep.* 8.2.3 (Roman clergy); 37.4.2; 56.3.1; 65.1.2. See also *Test.* III.117; PL 4.727C and 779A.

12. *Ep.* 8.2.1,2,3 and 8.3.4 (Roman clergy); 11.5.3; 12.2.2; 13.5.3; 14.1.1; 14.2.1.See also *Ep.* 80.1.3 (*stantes secundum fidei firmitatem*); *Unit.* 22; PL 4.516C (*stat...in fidei suae robore*).

13. *Ep.* 58.8.3; *Test.* III.117 (779A). Cyprian unites the two Greek verbs in a single *stetis* (Vulgate: *stare, state*).

14. See principally *Laps.* 4; PL 4.467B, where the *stantes fratres* are distinguished from the *martyres* and the *confessores*. The subject deals with believers who have persevered, without having had to confess their faith publicly. Cf. *Laps.* 2,3,13,22.

15. *Ep.* 56.2.1; 61.3.2; 76.7.3. See further *Unit.* 8 and 22.

16. *Unit.* 22 (cf. 8). See below n. 21. It should be noted that the subject is not flight, an image which is not found in Cyprian.

17. *Fortis et stabilis*: *Ep.* 11.8 (the *fiducia* of the *perseuerantes* as opposed to *lapsi*. 28.2.1; 67.8.1. Cf. *Ad Fortunatum* 13, PL 4.675B. — *Fortes et stabiles*: *Ep.* 6.1.2; 10.1.1. Cf. *Unit.* 2.

18. *In fide stabiles*: *Ep.* 10.4.4 (cf. Col. 1:23); *stabilitas in fide*: *Dom. or.* 15; PL 4.529B.

19. *Ep.* 12.1.3, quoting Rev. 2:10.

20. *Stabilis atque inconcussa*: *Ep.* 59.2.3 (*uirtus*); *Ad Donatum* 14, PL 4.220B (*tutela*). — *Stabilitas inconcussa*: *Ep.* 28.1.1 (note here, as in *Ep.* 59.2.3, the parallel with *robur immobile*; the associating of *stabilis* and *immobile* reminds one of Col. 1:23; cf. below n. 104.

21. *Stabilis*: *Laps.* 2 (*congressio*) and 13 (*mens*; as a parallel with *fides fortis*). — *Stabilitas*: *Ep.* 59.7.3 (with *solidari*, in reference to seed as opposed to straw). There is also *stabilitas solida* (*Ep.* 55.3.1 and *stabilitas gloriosa* 43.7.1, in connection with *perpetua firmitas*).

22. *Ep.* 28.2.1, 59.2.3; 59.7.3; 67.8.1. In *Ep.* 55.3.1 and *Unit.* 2 Cyprian refers to the house built on the rock (Mt. 7:24-25).

23. *Ad Fortunatum* 8, dealing directly with the subject of martyrdom. Note the quotation from Mt. 10:22 at the beginning.

24. *Ad Donatum* 14 (*tutela*) and 15 (*fiducia*).

25. *Ep.* 59.7.3: *nunquam ab eo Christo omnino discedere* characterizes the Church, in contrast with the schismatics, *quos uidemus non frumenti stabilitate solidari*.

26. In the Greek Orient this vocabulary is spontaneously employed by Chrysostom, *Adversus oppugnat. uit. mon.* III.13, in contrasting the *stantes* (faithful monks) and the *pesontes* (fallen monks).

27. He often uses them in speaking of spiritual values. See *Conl.* 9.2.1, *firma...uel stabilia perdurare* (virtuous practices); 9.2.3, *immobiliter...stabiliri* (the edifice of virtues); 10.8.5, *stabiliter...tenemus* (a prayer formula); 10.12, *stabiliter retinere* (the verse *Deus in adiutorium*); 10.14.T, *stabilitas cordis*; 10.14.1, *mentem stabilem...animae stabilem firmitatem*; 16.24, *caritas stabilis atque indisrupta*, etc.

28. Cassian, *Inst.* 7.9.1, *instabilitatis suae uiaticum*; 10.6, *instabilem...ac uagum*. The same words are used for various spiritual maladies. See *Inst.* 5.21.3, *peruagatio cordis instabilis*; 12.4.3, *instabilis ac nuta bundus* (Lucifer). *Conl.* 15.4, *uacuos...atque instabiles* (efforts without aim). *Conl.* 10.13.1, *animus...instabilis uagusque*, etc.

29. *Inst.* 4.1-4

30. Mt. 10:22 (cf. above n. 19), quoted by Cassian, *Inst.* 4.36.2.

31. *Inst.* 4.11.4 and 4.36.2, *ad finem usque*; 4.37, *usque ad finem uitae nostrae...usque ad extremum uitae.* Cf. *Inst.* 4.2, *usque ad incuruam senectutem*; 4.41, *perpetuo.* See also *Inst.* 12.28 and *Conl.* 18.6.3, quoting Phil. 2:8; *usque ad mortem* (with the embellishment in the second case: *usque ad finem*); *Conl.* 24.2.5, *usque in finem.*

32. *Inst.* 4.36.2 (*nuditas*; going on to speak of *humilitas ac patientia*); 4.37 (*Christi humilitas atque paupertas*).

33. *Inst.* 4.38, *perfectionem professum.* In *Inst.* 4.33, the subject of the "profession" remains indefinite (*quod professi sunt*).

34. *Conl.* 24.3-7.

35. *Inst.* 10.3. On the devil's efforts to lure a monk out of his cell on the pretext of good monks, see *Conl.* 1.20.5.

36. *Inst.* 10.23 (on the subject of the coenobium). Cf. *Inst.* 10.2.1, *horrorem loci, cellae fastidium;* 10.2.2, *loco...cella.*

37. See the previous note.

38. Colomba, *Reg. mon.* 8 (p. 136; 15-17 Walker).

39. Columba, *De octo uitiis principalibus,* publ. G.S.M. Walker, *Sancti Columbani Opera,* Dublin, 1957, p. 210, 30-31. The editor regards the work as genuine, with good reason (p. LXII), although thinking it right to relegate it to an Appendix.

40. RB 48.18: *frater acediosus, qui vacat otio aut fabulis.*

41. Cassian, *Inst.* 10.6; cf. RM 1.13-74.

42. *Conl.* 6.15

43. *Conl.* 7.23.3.

44. *Apophthegmata Patrum,* Arsenius 11; Hieraeas 1; Paphnucius 5.

45. *Vitae Patrum.* V, 7.24,30,34: *Sede in cella tua.* See PL 73.897C; 900D); 901C. The same instruction is given in other words (*de cella non exeas*), in *V. Patr.* V, 7.27, which repeats Arsenius' apophthegm.

46. See *V. Patr.* V, 7.7,15,26,28,32,33-39,47. Cf. *V. Patr.* V,1.1; 2.1 & 9.

47. *V. Patr.* V, 7.15 and 36. — Paschasius, *Apopht.* 97.1, in J.G. Freire, *A Versao latina por Pascasio de Dume dos Apophthegmata Patrum,* vol. I, Coimbra, 1971, p. 328. The putting together of the two apophthegms (of Paschasius) appears artificial. In reality, the first one (Syncletica 6) is coenobitic, the second (N 204) anchoritic.

48. This *frequenter* betrays the apophthegm (preceding note).

49. *RIVP* 2.27. Cf. Lk. 11:8.

50. *RIVP* 4.4-6. Cf. 1 Tim. 5:12.

51. *RIVP* 4.7-13.

52. 2 *RP* 10. The same too in RB 67.7.

53. 2 *RP* 29.

54. Eusebius Gallicanus, *Hom.* 38.4.

55. *Hom.* 38.2.

56. *Hom.* 38.4 (cf. 2).

57. *Hom.* 39.2-3.

58. *Hom.* 40.2 (the time spent in religion) and 3 (the life in community on the island).

59. *Hom.* 40.3. This *in loco uocationis nostrae* (line 120), which is found also in *Hom.* 38.4 (line 118: *de loco ad quem te dominus tuus uocauerat*), recalls 1 Cor. 7:20.

60. *Hom.* 40.7. Cf. Gal. 2:2. Phil. 2:16.

61. *RMac.* 25-28.

62. 3 *RP* 4,8,9,10,12.

63. *3 RP* 14.

64. Ferreolus, *Reg.* 6, here quoting, as too would Benedict, RB 61.13-14, the "Golden Rule" from the Gospel. See also Ferreolus, *Reg.* 20.

65. Leo, *Ep.* 1.1 (Aquileus): *instabilitatem suam per diuersa circumferant, amantes semper errare* (ecclesiastics converted from Pelagianism); *Ep.* 42 (Arles): *uagum et semper erroneum...ecclesias circuire* (a pseudo-Roman deacon). One thinks of Augustine, *Op. mon.* 36 (wandering monks); *En. Ps.* 132.3 (donatist "circoncellions"). Leo uses *stare* as well for denoting, like Cyprian, those who "hold fast" in the orthodox faith (*Ep.* 75.2, cf. 1 Cor. 16:13; *Ep.* 105.1, 147.3; 164.5). See also *Ep.* 18 (*stabilitas*: the lack of promotion to which are condemned those ecclesiastics reconverted from heresy); 59.1 (*instabiles*); 104.3 (*stabilis*); 140 (*instabiles*).

66. RM Ths 45-46. Cf. RB Prol. 45-50.

67. See A. de Vogüé: *La Règle de saint Benoît*, vol. VII, Paris, 1977, pp. 33-74.

68. RM 4.10.

69. RM 5.10. Therefore *perseuerantia* is not only opposed to apostasy but also to "gyrovagy."

70. RM 6:1-2: *Officina uero monasterium est, in qua...opus diuinae artis diligent custodia perseuerando operari potest.*

71. RM 10.52-60 = RB 7.35-43.

72. RM 10.52-53 = RB 7.35-36.

73. RM 10.56 = RB 7.39, quoting Rom. 8:37.

74. RM 7.57-65 (see 7.59: *uelutin martyric patienter*). Cf. our book *La communauté et l'abbé dans la Règle de saint Benoît*, Paris, 1961, pp. 244-246.

75. RM 10.53 = RB 7.36, quoting Mt. 10:22 (or Mt. 24:13). These words of Christ were already underlying RM 4.10 (*perseuerantia usque in finem*).

76. Cassian, *Inst.* 4.36.2 (cf. above n. 25).

77. Rev. 2:10; Phil. 2:8 (quoted in RM 10.49 = RB 7.34).

78. Acts 2:42.

79. 2 Jn. 9. The opposite (*qui recedit*) reminds one of RM Ths 46 = RB Prol. 50: *ab ipsius numquam magisterio discedentes*, which recalls more specifically Cyprian, *Ep.* 63.10.2; *a diuino magisterio non recedamus.*

80. RM 79.28: *se monasterio usque ad mortem perseuerando contradant.*

81. RM 87.35-37 (cf. 87.58: *perseuerantia monasterii*).

82. RM 90.93: *ut uel occasione rerum suarum ad Dei disciplinam in monasterio permanentes retineantur discipuli.*

83. RM 90.95: *perseuerantia calciat et uestit, discessus restituit debitas monasterio res et si cupit, abscedit.*

84. RB Prol 50; 7.35-43.

85. RB 4.78: *Officina uero ubi haec omnia diligenter operemur claustra sunt monasterii et stabilitas in congregatione.* These *claustra* (*monasterii*) are to be compared with the (*corporis*) *clusura* of RM 6.2. Originally applied to the monk's body, the image is transferred by Benedict to the monastic building. Cf. *La Règle de saint Benoît*, vol. IV (*Sources Chrétiennes* 184), pp. 221-223.

86. RM 89.T-1 (*firmare...stabilitas...perseuerantia...firmitate*) and 34 (*stabilitatem monasterio...frangat,* on the subject of the written deed by which the professed monk gives his goods to the monastery).

87. RM 89.8.

88. In contrast to RM Ths 46, where *usque ad mortem* is added to *in monasterio.* — In *La Règle de saint Benoît* vol. VI (*Sources Chrétiennes* 186), p. 1327, we linked *in monasterio tuo* (RM 89.8) with the *stabilitas* which is promised RB 58.17. This rapprochement is valid only for the element of place in stability, not for the time factor.

89. RM 89.17-23. Cf. 87.33-37.

90. RB 58.17-18.

91. Caesarius, *Reg. uirg.* 2: *Si qua...uoluerit introire...usque ad mortem suam de monasterio non egrediatur, nec in basilicam ubi ostium esse uidetur.* Cf. 50.

92. *Reg. uirg.* 59 and 73.

93. *Reg. uirg.* 58 (*Recapitulatio*).

94. Caesarius, *Reg. mon.* 1: *In primis siquis ad conuersionem uenerit, ea conditione excipiatur ut usque mortem suam ibi perseueret.* In the final portion (*Reg. mon.* 26 = *Gaudete...*), containing a passage from the Epistle *Vereor,* Caesarius quotes Mt. 10:22, but this "enduring to the end" is rather a matter of perpetual conversion in the moral sphere, as for Cassian, than one of stability. Caesarius at any rate relies here as in the *Reg. uirg.* 49 upon Cassian, *Inst.* 4.36.2, whose characteristic introduction he copies (*non qui coeperit, sed...*) as well as its accompanying scriptural reminiscences).

95. With regard to Caesarius, the fact has to be taken into account that the monks are probably not subjected to such absolute enclosure as the nuns.

96. Aurelian, *Reg. mon.* 1 = *Reg. uirg.* 1 repeats the expression from Caesarius, *Reg. uirg.* 2; however the *de monasterio egredi* has perhaps changed in meaning, for the "door" is no longer mentioned and the rule applies to men just as much as to women. See also *Reg. mon.* 46.

97. Isidore, *Reg.* 4.2: *nisi prius professione aut uerbi aut scripti teneantur.*

98. *Ibid.*: *Omnis conuersus non est recipiendus in monasterio nisi prius ibi se scriptis sponderit permansurum.*

99. Called to mind in *Orig.* 9.3.40 (PL 82.73).

100. This appears at first sight an erudite reminiscence, since the legions no longer existed in Isidore's period, nor had they for a long time, and he lived under the Visigoths' domination. However it may be that this eminently well-read writer introduced the regulation through the influence of something he had read.

101. Fructuosus, *Reg.* 22 (21 Campos): *accipiet pactum eius...in quo ita se isdem conuertens alligabit, ut omnis se instituta coenobi mente deuota profiteatur implere. Neque ea ullo umquam tempore uiolare, neque adstrictione coenobii quam expetit polliceatur ullatenus euagari.* This commitment precedes the year of novitiate prescribed above (*Reg.* 21; 20 Campos). On this subject, we were mistaken in writing (in *La Règle de saint Benoît*, vol. VI, p. 1348) that Fructuosus "allows for no reduction in this whole-year period." It is in fact only the *Regula communis* 18 which prescribes an *annus integer* without fail. — The *euagari* in this passage is found again in *Reg.* 23 (22.439 Campos): *nec liceat monachum foris claustri coenobii proprii longius euagari,* etc., where it clearly refers to enclosure, not to stability. Cf. Isidore, *Reg.* 1.3: the garden in the cloister *quatenus...nulla occasione exterius euagentur.*

102. *Pactum,* in *S. Leandro - S. Fructuoso - S. Isidoro, Reglas monasticas de la Espana visigoda,* ed. J. Campos, I. Rocca, Madrid, 1971 (BAC 321), pp. 210.696-211.705.

103. *Reg. com.* 2,4,18,20.

104. Gregory, *Dial.* III.16.9. Cf. Theodoret, *HR* 26.10.

105. 1 S. 6:14.

106. An allusion to what is before. The field of Joshua (Jesus) represents the joys of the anticipated vision of heaven.

107. Gregory, *In I Regum* III:122.

108. Cf. our article "Les vues de Grégoire le Grand sur la vie religieuse dans son Commentaire des Rois," in *Studia monastica* 20 (1978), pp. 17-63 (see p. 40).

109. Mt. 10:22.

110. 1 Cor. 16:13.

111. 1 Pet. 5:9.

112. Rev. 2:10.

113. *Stabilis* itself appears in Col. 1:23 (above n. 16); 1 Cor. 15:58: *stabiles estote et immobiles.* This latter adjective is used by Cyprian *Ep.* 8.2.1; 8.3.4 (Roman clergy); 28.1.1; 59.2.3; *Unit.* 2.2.

114. Palladius, *Hist. Laus.* 18.29 = Heraclides, *Parad.* 6, PL 74.276D.

115. J. Leclercq, *Aux sources de la spiritualité occidentale,* vol. I, Paris, 1964, pp. 35-90 (*Monachisme et pérégrination*); Id., *Vie érémitique et itinerante,* in *Les moines chrétiens face aux religions d'Asie.* Bangalore, 1973, Vanves, 1974, pp. 216-218; A. Guillaumont, *Aux origines du monachisme*

chrétien, Bellefontaine, 1979 (Spiritualité orientale 30), pp. 89-116, (*dépaysment comme forme d'ascèse dans le monachisme ancien*).
116. Cassian, *Inst* . 4.3.1: they came *orationis causa.*
117. See for example Palladius, *Hist. Laus.* 35.3-4 (visit to John of Lyco); Cyril of Scythopolis, *Vita Euthymii* 5,7,25,39 and *Vita Sabae* 11,22,27: they go off to wander in the desert throughout Lent, starting in January; *Vie de sainte Marie l'Egyptienne* 6: the same practice, restricted to the period of Lent properly speaking; *Vie des Pères du Jura*, p. 44-50 (Romanus and Palladius at Agaune) and 153-156 (two brothers on pilgrimage to Rome and elsewhere for two years; they bring back some relics).
118. RM 95.17-21; RB 66.6-7 (cf. 67.3-5). The Master and Benedict are mindful of the ideal of absolute enclosure suggested in *Historia monachorum* 17 (the monastery of Abbot Isidore).
119. Such as Syria and Ireland (cf. above n. 106).
120. Cf. A. Guillaumont, *art. cit.*, pp. 106-111. To the two exceptions cited by the author (Bisario and Serapio), may be added the "anchorites" or wandering hermits mentioned by Sulpicius Severus *Dial.* I, 15-16 (cf. 18).
121. Cassian, *Conl.* 24.3-6.
122. On Benedictine stability and its antecedents, one may also consult B. Steidle, "Das Versprechen der 'Bestandigkeit,' des 'Tugend-Wandels' und des 'Gehorsams' in der Regel St. Benedikts," in *Erbe und Auftrag* 36 (1960), which refers to M. Rothenhausler's work; G. Veloso, "Church Ordinances in Augustine's Africa Touching on Monastic Stability," in *Philippiniana Sacra* (Manila, 1972), pp. 89-113, giving a sample of the research condensed in his unpublished Roman thesis; J. Leclercq, "Autour de la Règle de saint Benoît," in *Collectanea Cisterciensia* 37 (1975), pp. 167-204, which refers to G. Veloso's thesis (see 197-204); (it is because of an oversight, corrected in the German translation of the article, that page 198 states that G. Veloso was our guide in the commentary on the RB; in actual fact we participated in the development of his thesis by giving him the advice he requested).

Word and Spirit, 17 — 1995
Monastic On-Going Formation

To reserve your copy, order from:

St. Bede's Publications
P.O. Box 545
Petersham, Massachusetts 01366-0545

Standing orders available

Still Available:

Word and Spirit, 2 — 1980
In honor of Sts. Benedict
    and Scholastica

Word and Spirit, 3 — 1981
On the Holy Spirit and on Prayer

Word and Spirit, 5 — 1983
Christology

Word and Spirit, 7 — 1985
St. Bede: A Tribute

Word and Spirit, 8 — 1986
Process Theology and the
    Christian Doctrine of God

Word and Spirit, 9 — 1987
St. Augustine

Word and Spirit, 10 — 1988
Mary in Monasticism

Word and Spirit, 11 — 1989
Women in Monasticism

Word and Spirit, 12 — 1990
St. Bernard

Word and Spirit, 13 — 1991
Asceticism Today

Word and Spirit, 14 — 1992
Aspects of Monasticism
    in America

Word and Spirit, 15 — 1993
The Spiritual Journey